"Conrad's first book—*Daring Devotion*—was a gift to God's people. Can I suggest that *Daring Dependence* is an even greater gift? These glimpses into the lives of gospel servants, in a wide range of circumstances, illustrate God's true faithfulness to those who depend upon Him. Men and women of various nationalities, backgrounds, and ministries show us what it means to depend upon God in weakness. Insightful comments and reflection questions ending each day's reading effectively guide us to a daring dependence upon Christ. *Daring Dependence* is a powerful tool of encouragement for all those laboring in God's harvest."

—FORREST MCPHAIL, missionary to Cambodia and regional director for Asia, Australia, and Oceania, Gospel Fellowship Association Missions

"The world suffers from an annoying surplus of social media influencers who choreograph adventures to serve their vapid aim of winning themselves more followers. A Christian's adventures are better because the mission is better: to follow Jesus and win *Him* more followers. Conrad's enthralling snapshots and well-aimed reflections foment in me the kind of dependent daring I need more of each day."

—DAVID HOSAFLOOK, missionary to Albania, author, and founder and executive director of the Institute for Albanian and Protestant Studies

"Encouraging and convicting! Powerful missionary stories with applications for my daily life. These men and women were not great and mighty people but dependent people, trusting in the same great and mighty God we serve today."

—HANNAH BENDER, missionary nurse and director of educational services, Medical Missions Outreach

"In some ways, this missions devotional could serve as a history of Anglo-American missions of the past two centuries. Beginning with William Carey, that iconic missional figure of the late eighteenth-century, it takes the reader on a month-long journey of the way that 'great things' (to cite Carey) have been attempted for God by men and women who were flat-out dependent on our glorious Lord. Informative, stirring, challenging, it is a needed reflection—not only for anyone thinking of being a vocational missionary, but also for those who wish to support such in prayer, fasting, and finances."

—MICHAEL A. G. HAYKIN, author and professor of church history, The Southern Baptist Theological Seminary

"These well-written vignettes from eighteenth- and nineteenth-century missionary history draw the reader in to reveal God's glory, power, and saving grace among the nations. They serve to instruct and motivate a new generation of missionaries, and they also serve the people who pray and send them to proclaim the glorious gospel once proclaimed by William Carey, Jean Dye Johnson, Jim Elliot, and John Stam. In these devotions, you will see glimpses of grace, the sovereign power of God, and the sure advance of the gospel in the face of the impossible. I recommend this resource for your family devotions, for distribution to your church, and as a basis for Bible study that will fuel a mission mindset in your church. This is one of the best-written mission devotionals I have been privileged to read. I have benefited from each page."

—PHIL HUNT, church planter in Zambia, president of Central Africa Baptist University, and Africa field director for IBMGlobal

"It is the Lord of the Harvest Who calls missionaries. It is the church who sends and supports them. But it is other missionaries, both past and present, who inspire them. In *Daring Dependence,* as in *Daring Devotion,* M. R. Conrad has given us heaping portions of inspiration through riveting missionary stories and careful biblical teaching. Nothing short of exceptional!"

—CHRIS ANDERSON, vice president for global advancement, Biblical Ministries Worldwide and author with Church Works Media

"Young people today need godly heroes to provide patterns and purpose in serving Christ. M. R. Conrad has produced another wonderful resource introducing young people and adults to the lives of such faithful servants. *Daring Dependence* offers snapshots of men and women who, in their weakness, trusted the Lord to strengthen and sustain them as they successfully advanced the gospel of Jesus Christ. Like Elijah in James 5:17, they also had 'a nature like ours' and 'prayed earnestly.' This book will challenge you to heed the words of William Carey: 'Expect great things from God, and attempt great things for God.'"

—KEN ENDEAN, pastor of Tri-City Baptist Church in Chandler, Arizona, board chair of International Baptist College and Seminary, and board president for International Baptist Missions

"Biography has been described as 'life without theory.' The power of biography cannot be overstated because it is rooted in reality. In his missions devotional, *Daring Dependence,* M. R. Conrad masterfully tells brief yet compelling biographical stories of missionaries whose lives have exemplified what it means to serve Christ with daring dependence. Each daily story will challenge the reader to trust the Lord in courageous ways."

—PATRICK ODLE, president, Baptist Mid-Missions

DARING
DEPENDENCE

A 31-DAY JOURNEY
WITH THOSE WHO FOUND
THEIR STRENGTH IN GOD

M. R. CONRAD

Published by Church Works Media
FIRST EDITION 2022
Editing by Joe Tyrpak, Chris Anderson, and Abby Huffstutler
Cover design, illustrations, and layout by Erik Peterson with Joe Tyrpak

ISBN 978-1-7343978-8-8 (Paperback)
www.mrconrad.net
www.churchworksmedia.com

TABLE OF CONTENTS

CHRONOLOGICAL
TABLE OF CONTENTS

WHERE DEPENDENCE ON GOD LED

1 William Carey	12 Samuel J. Mills	23 Robert Moffat
2 Henry Nott	13 Samuel Zwemer	24 Mary Moffat
3 Ernie Presswood	14 Hannah Marshman	25 Xi Shengmo
4 Lilias Trotter	15 John Williams	26 Xi Shimu
5 James Gilmour	16 Mary Williams	27 Jesse Irvin Overholtzer
6 C. T. Studd	17 Amy Carmichael	28 Evangeline French
7 Jean Dye Johnson	18 D. E. Hoste	29 Ann Judson
8 Oswald Chambers	19 D. L. Moody	30 John Stam
9 William Ward	20 Raymond Lull	31 Jim Elliot
10 Maria Dyer Taylor	21 James Chalmers	
11 J. Hudson Taylor	22 Gladys Aylward	

CHART OF INFLUENCE

Raymond Lull (c. 1232–1315)
William Carey (1761–1834)
Hannah Marshman (1767–1847)
William Ward (1769–1823)
Henry Nott (1774–1844)
Samuel J. Mills (1783–1818)
Ann Judson (1789–1826)
Mary Williams (1789–1852)
Robert Moffat (1795–1883)
Mary Moffat (1795–1871)
John Williams (1796–1839)
J. Hudson Taylor (1832–1905)
Xi Shengmo (c. 1836–1896)
Maria Dyer Taylor (1837–1870)
D. L. Moody (1837–1899)
Xi Shimu (c. 1839–c. 1920)
James Chalmers (1841–1901)
James Gilmour (1843–1891)
Lilias Trotter (1853–1928)
C. T. Studd (1860–1931)
D. E. Hoste (1861–1946)
Amy Carmichael (1867–1951)
Samuel Zwemer (1867–1952)
Evangeline French (1869–1960)
Oswald Chambers (1874–1917)
Jesse Irvin Overholtzer (1877–1955)
Gladys Aylward (1902–1970)
John Stam (1907–1934)
Ernie Presswood (1908–1946)
Jean Dye Johnson (1920–2012)
Jim Elliot (1927–1956)

JOURNEY BRIEFING

"O God, You are my God;
Early will I seek You; My soul thirsts for You;
My flesh longs for You
In a dry and thirsty land
Where there is no water.
So I have looked for You in the sanctuary,
To see Your power and Your glory.
Because Your lovingkindness is better than life,
My lips shall praise You. . . .
When I remember You on my bed,
I meditate on You in the night watches.
Because You have been my help,
Therefore in the shadow of Your wings I will rejoice.
My soul follows close behind You;
Your right hand upholds me."

—PSALM 63:1–8

Daring Dependence. What an odd combination of words. How do these two terms make sense together? We equate *daring* with strength and audacity, but we usually view *dependence* as weakness. Yet, as Psalm 63 and the true stories in this missions devotional show, the hand of the Almighty God upholds and empowers those who depend on Him, the Source of all strength.

I invite you to embark on a journey toward greater dependence on God and to read this book as an illustration of the truths of Psalm 63. This psalm provides a glimpse into the spiritual life of David, whom God describes as "a man after My own heart" (Acts 13:22). As David navigated his own journey of dependence on God, he fought bears and lions, defeated giants, and conquered Israel's enemies in the strength of the Lord. How did he access this strength? Through his walk with God. The Lord was with him (1 Samuel 18:12, 14, 28; 2 Samuel 5:10). Though he stands out as Israel's most notable ruler, David was a flawed man and an imperfect leader. However, David's passion for the Lord, sensitivity to the Holy Spirit, and desire to please God shined through his life. His example inspires those who hear his story and read his poetry.

Throughout church history, men and women like David have sought to live after God's own heart, drawing near Him, growing in their dependence on Him, and serving in His power. This book highlights thirty-one snapshots of God's servants. Like David, they had their faults. Some of their decisions and beliefs could well be questioned by modern Christians. However, their passion for God, reliance on His strength, and determination to spread the true gospel of salvation by grace through faith make them stand out as examples for us today.

Before becoming a missionary to Ecuador, Elisabeth Elliot found such an example in Amy Carmichael. As Elliot read Carmichael's biography and personal writings, Elliot grew to feel like she knew this missionary to India from the previous generation. She wrote,

> Amy Carmichael became for me what some now call a role
> model. She was far more than that. She was my first spiritual
> mother. She showed me the shape of godliness. For a time,
> I suppose, I thought she must be perfect, and that was good
> enough for me. As I grew up I knew she could not have been
> perfect, and that was better, for it meant that I might possibly
> walk in her footprints. If we demand perfect models we will
> have, except for the Son of man Himself, none at all.[1]

Like Elliot, we have much to learn from the imperfect-yet-faithful models who came before us.

Didactic truth informs us, but lived truth inspires us. Yes, we must hear the truth from God's Word, but we also need to see the truth in action. We benefit from flesh-and-blood examples that show us what walking by faith looks like throughout the journey of life. For this reason (and many others in God's infinite wisdom), God often teaches His people through stories. His first written revelation, the book of Genesis, is truth taught through narratives of actual historical events. Of all the genres in the Old Testament—narrative, poetry, wisdom, law, and prophecy—narrative is most common, comprising over forty percent of the Bible's first thirty-nine books. The trend continues in the New Testament where the first five books are predominantly narrative. God uses true stories to communicate and illustrate His truth.

Though inspired Scripture ceased with the book of Revelation, God's work through men and women did not. Missionary biographies continue this story, challenging and discipling us as we read them. They open our eyes, not just to countries and cultures we have never seen, but also to God's continued work in this world. We marvel as God uses ordinary people, sustains them through extreme situations, and snatches victory from the jaws of defeat. We become aware of factors that the subjects of the biographies never knew, like how God worked after their deaths. As we learn, we take courage that what we see today is not the end of the story.

In addition, these historical examples help us learn that we cannot make a difference for God on our own. A fruitful life of service for God is never a solo, independent journey. As this missions devotional will show, those whom God has used throughout the ages consistently point to the same source of strength—dependence on God.

What is dependence on God? The Bible describes this concept from different angles, including walking by faith (2 Corinthians 5:7), walking in the Spirit (Galatians 5:16, 25), being filled with the Spirit (Ephesians 5:18), abiding in Christ (John 15:1-16), and waiting on God (Isaiah 40:31). Since creation, God has sought men and women who desire to walk with Him (Genesis 5:24). Those who walk with God follow His direction and learn to depend on Him.

Dependence on God comes out of a close relationship with God as we recognize our utter need for His empowerment. Only God can transform us into His holy likeness. Only He can strengthen us to obey His commands. Only He can empower us to persevere faithfully in a sin-broken world. Only He can use us to bear lasting fruit. To put it more simply, we rely on God's strength to be, to do, to overcome, and to make a difference for Him.

Dependence on God lives in the reality of John 15:5: "Without Me you can do nothing."[2] It triumphs in the hope of Philippians

4:13: "I can do all things through Christ who strengthens me." We express dependence upon God when we give top priority to our daily time with God in His Word and when we promptly confess and forsake our sins. We demonstrate our reliance on Him when we "pray without ceasing" as part of our normal reaction to life's ups and downs (1 Thessalonians 5:17). This dependence grows as we follow God step by step. As a result, we do what we would not have attempted on our own. The lives highlighted in this book reveal what God can do in and through those who dare to depend on His strength.

This book will take you on a journey of thirty-one readings— one for each day of a month. My hope is that you will use these devotionals to supplement your personal time with God. Nothing can take the place of the daily reading of Scripture. Therefore, I have designed this missions devotional to point you to God's Word and to a closer walk with its Author.

I have arranged each chapter of *Daring Dependence* in a somewhat topical manner, hoping for the reader to make connections between people, places, and events. However, if you would prefer to read chronologically, please refer to the Chronological Table of Contents. I have also included a world map showing where those in this book served.

Additionally, please note the Chart of Influence just preceding this preface that shows how Christians of the past, through their examples and biographies, have influenced subsequent generations to follow Christ. This chart can also be compared to a similar diagram in my earlier book, *Daring Devotion*. Together, the two charts provide a greater perspective on the interconnectedness of God's work and workers through the centuries.

Beware! The testimonies in this book may spark your spiritual imagination to be more and do more for God. The Holy Spirit may use these biographical examples to convict you to walk closer with Him. You may even begin to wonder what God could do with your life if you learned to rely more on Him. Do you dare read on?

THE STARTING POINT

"Therefore if any man be in Christ, he is a new creature: old things are passed away; behold, all things are become new."
—2 CORINTHIANS 5:17

James Wilson woke up chained to a corpse again. Yet another of his fellow prisoners had perished in the night. As he lay dehydrated on the filthy floor of the Srirangapatna dungeon in southern India, Wilson knew his chances of survival were slim. Yet, no prayer escaped his lips.

During the early 1780s, the British fought the French along the shores of India. Twenty-two-year-old Wilson joined the fight as an experienced British sailor. When he was just fifteen years old, he had stood with the British at Bunker Hill in the American War for Independence. Then in India, Wilson had risen to captain his own ship. For months, he smuggled weapons and supplies past the French blockade. However, on June 15, 1782, a heavily armed frigate forced him to run up the white flag. When the French sold their British prisoners to a local ally, the sultan Hyder Ali, young Wilson's fate was sealed.

The night before his transfer to Ali's fort, Wilson plotted his escape. Under the cover of darkness, he slipped away during the changing of the guard. He leaped from the fortress wall, dropping forty feet to the river below, and swam to freedom.[1] Over forty miles, Wilson eluded capture, keeping in the shadows of the Indian jungles and fording alligator-infested rivers. He hoped to discover a British camp or maybe the Danish settlement. Instead, when Wilson was just a few miles from safety, Ali's men captured him.

Twenty-three months later, Wilson still languished in Ali's prison. Exposed to the tropical elements and fed only a small bowl of dirty rice per day, his body withered to the point that his chains would sometimes slip off. His long hair turned gray and then fell out. Further weakened by dysentery, Wilson cursed his fate. Death visited his prison daily. Only thirty-two of the 112 inmates would survive.[2] Though Wilson scoffed at the very idea of divine providence, God spared him.

A British victory in late April 1784 ended Wilson's imprisonment. After he regained his health, the twenty-four-year-old—who now looked like an old man—returned to the sea. He started over as a mate but soon earned promotions until he once again captained his own ship. By age thirty-six, Captain Wilson had amassed a fortune and retired to England.

On his voyage home, Wilson sailed with Dr. John Thomas. Thomas had served as the first medical missionary to India and would soon convince William Carey to accompany him on his return trip. The doctor boldly challenged the captain with the

gospel. However, Wilson rejected God's grace with such vehe-
mence that Thomas believed there was more hope of leading one
of the Muslim sailors to Christ than their profane British captain.

Wilson's antagonism to Christianity continued into his retire-
ment in the quaint Hampshire village of Horndean. Over the next
two years, he gained a reputation as a wealthy gentleman and a
skeptic. He ignored the Christian testimony of his niece who
served as his housekeeper, and he reveled in his intellectual triumphs over his neighbor Captain Sims, who also attempted to
share Christ.

One day, Sims introduced Wilson to his pastor, John Griffin.
Wilson welcomed the challenge: "I am glad of the opportunity
to converse on the evidences of the so-called Divine origin of the
Christian Scriptures, and I never met the clergyman yet whom I
could not foil in a quarter of an hour."[3] After three hours, Wilson
had not yet confounded Griffin. When they suspended their discussion, Wilson told Sims, "He has said some things I shall never
forget." That night, as Griffin calmly addressed Wilson's objec-
tions, Griffin pointed him to the gospel of Jesus Christ, the only
remedy for sin. The gospel Griffin explained to Wilson is the same
gospel God offers each person alive today.

The gospel message begins before the dawn of human history.
God created a perfect world. Genesis 1:31 reports that "God
saw everything that He had made, and indeed it was very good."
Perfect human beings lived in harmony with one another, with the
nature around them, and, most importantly, with their Creator.

Then, sin shattered this brief utopia and severed humans' relationship with God. The Bible explains that "through one man sin
entered the world, and death through sin, and thus death spread to

all men, because all sinned" (Romans 5:12). So ever since the first sin, each person is a sinner by birth and by choice (Romans 3:23). Each one of us has chosen wrong instead of right (1 John 5:17). Even when we have tried our best to hit whatever target of righteousness we prefer, we miss the mark. We do what we should not do, and we do not do what we should. We go our own way instead of the way God intended for us (Isaiah 53:6). We reject the God Who made us and loves us.

Going our own way leads to destruction: "There is a way that seems right to a man, but its end is the way of death" (Proverbs 16:25). Death is separation and comes in three stages—spiritual, physical, and eternal. First, we are separated from God in this world. In our spiritual blindness, we have no idea how lost we are without Him. We wander in darkness with no vital connection to God. Second, our body dies physically. Without the power of the gospel, all hope of salvation dies in the grave with us (Hebrews 9:27). Third, we experience eternal death, separated forever from God and everyone else in the torment of hell (Revelation 20:15). God warns us that "the wages of sin is death" (Romans 6:23). But there is hope.

Even though we are separated from God because of our sin, our Creator reaches down to us. Over two thousand years ago, Jesus came to earth. Angels announced how He would enter the world—a virgin would conceive (Isaiah 7:14; Matthew 1:23). Though He is God, the Creator, He would become human and dwell with His creation (John 1:1, 14). His name would be Jesus, meaning "Savior," and He would save people from the separation and death our sin brings on us (Matthew 1:21).

During His earthly ministry, Jesus—through His words, His fulfilled prophecy, and His unmistakable miracles—proved His deity. However, as God foresaw, the people He created rejected their God and Savior. Even the depraved anger that murdered Jesus Christ on the cross fulfilled God's plan. Jesus had come to die in our place. He died so that we could live.

Three days after His death, Jesus came back to life. His resurrection proved His power to save. Only a living Savior can save dying people, and so Jesus assures us, "I am the resurrection and the life. He who believes in Me, though he may die, he shall live" (John 11:25).

God offers us life through the gospel. John 3:16 explains this good news: "For God so loved the world that He gave His only begotten Son, that whoever believes in Him should not perish but have everlasting life." This is the gospel! Belief in Jesus Christ's death and resurrection is the turning point from death unto life.

But the gospel demands a response: Will you accept or reject Jesus' death and resurrection for you?

Rejecting salvation comes in many forms. Some are overt—skepticism and ridicule, like James Wilson. Most are quieter. We smile and put it off. We repeat the lie that all roads lead to God. We attempt to earn salvation by trying to do right and not harm others. Yet, each of these quieter responses is still a passive rejection of Jesus Christ.

Titus 3:5 says, "Not by works of righteousness which we have done, but according to His mercy He saved us." The only response to the gospel that results in rescue from eternal death is forsaking your own way, accepting God's mercy, and trusting Jesus Christ alone. There is no other way: "Nor is there salvation in any other, for there is no other name under heaven given among men by which we must be saved" (Acts 4:12).

God calls you to "repent and believe the gospel" (Mark 1:15). Repent by admitting your sin and turning from your own efforts to please God. Believe by trusting completely in Christ's death as the punishment for your sin. Accept His grace—His salvation is a free gift that you do not deserve (Ephesians 2:8–9). Will you receive His remedy for your sins and be made right with God?

Wilson's and Griffin's discussion that night in 1795 focused on these gospel truths. As Wilson prepared to leave, Griffin challenged his new friend: "If you reject the remedy God has provided, remember there is no other, and you may be finally wrong and finally miserable."[4] In the following days, those words echoed in Wilson's mind. For the first time, the retired sea captain opened the Bible to consider its claims without trying to attack them. He began attending Griffin's church under the guise of driving his niece's carriage there. As he heard the teaching of Romans 8, Wilson saw the hand of God in the events of his life. What Wilson had assumed to be luck or his own skill in surviving so many dangers he now realized was the preserving work of a loving heavenly Father.

Wilson experienced what John Newton, another retired sea captain, had put to verse just over two decades before:

> Amazing grace! How sweet the sound;
> That saved a wretch like me!
> I once was lost, but now am found;
> Was blind, but now I see.

'Twas grace that taught my heart to fear,
And grace my fears relieved;
How precious did that grace appear
The hour I first believed.

Through many dangers, toils, and snares,
I have already come;
'Tis grace hath brought me safe thus far,
And grace will lead me home.

Captain James Wilson humbled himself, admitted his sin, and trusted Jesus Christ as his Savior. He told Griffin, "I have no language to express the happiness I now feel; and the gratitude I owe to God, I hope, will be expressed in the life I have yet to live by my zeal in the service of God bearing some proportion to that which I have manifested in the service of Satan."[5] Wilson was a changed man.

Salvation by grace through faith is the starting point for a new life. Wilson grew in the Lord. He broke off sinful habits. He sought to dedicate his talents and abilities to serve God. But what could a landlocked sea captain do for Christ? The answer came as Wilson read an article about the London Missionary Society (LMS) in the *Evangelical Magazine*.

Just one year earlier, the LMS had formed to obey the Great Commission. William Carey's recent writings and daring venture to India had shined a spotlight on this long-neglected command of Christ: "But you shall receive power when the Holy Spirit has come upon you; and you shall be witnesses to Me in Jerusalem, and in all Judea and Samaria, and to the end of the earth" (Acts 1:8). In Wilson's day, the end of the earth was the South Pacific, and the LMS was recruiting missionaries to be the first gospel witnesses in these scattered islands. But they lacked a sea captain.

Wilson immediately saw how God could use his skills in this pioneer effort. The veteran sea captain volunteered to join the mission without pay. When he was accepted, Wilson sold his home and helped the LMS purchase an ocean-worthy ship, the *Duff*. When the first team of missionaries was ready, Wilson sailed them to Tahiti and beyond.

The testimony of Captain James Wilson's salvation and transformation is not unique. The story of each of the people highlighted in this book begins at the same place—the gospel of Jesus Christ. Long before these men and women found their strength in God, they first believed the gospel. The life-changing work of the gospel launched the daring dependence that empowered their service for God.

Have you begun your relationship with God through Jesus Christ? Have you believed on Him for salvation from the punishment for your sin? The gospel is your starting point.

GOD, MY ALL-SUFFICIENT PORTION

*"I feel that it is good to commit my Soul, my Body, and my All
into the hands of God. Then the World appears little,
the Promises great, and God an all-sufficient Portion."*
—WILLIAM CAREY, MISSIONARY TO INDIA (1761-1834)

*"My flesh and my heart fail;
But God is the strength of my heart and my portion forever."*
—PSALM 73:26

William Carey's heart raced as he leaned against the railing of the *Kron Princess Maria*. The winds and tides had finally allowed the Danish ship to enter the Bay of Bengal on November 11, 1793. In the distance, Carey caught his first glimpse of the shores of India. He hoped it would not be his last. Beside Carey, Dr. John Thomas fidgeted. On his last stint in India, Thomas had incurred outstanding debts—debts he had failed to mention to his new coworkers. Soon, a flotilla of smaller boats surrounded the ship, their onboard hawkers clamoring to sell fish and other goods to the foreigners.

As the ship entered the Hooghly River on its way upstream to Kolkata (formerly Calcutta), thirty-two-year-old Carey, his wife Dorothy, his children, his sister-in-law, and Dr. Thomas kept alert. Before reaching the dock and the required inspection, they slipped into a smaller boat which whisked them away. The British East India Company patrolled the harbor and sought to turn away any foreigners who could potentially interfere with their profit. Soon, the new arrivals mingled with the locals in a bustling market. The first missionaries of a new era had arrived on their field.[1]

Though safely past the watchful eye of the British East India Company, Carey's difficulties had just begun. Almost immediately, he discovered that daily expenses would far exceed their estimates. Then, his coworker, Dr. Thomas, panicked as creditors learned of his return to Kolkata. Thomas took the team's remaining money and used it to set up a medical practice for European colonials to pay off his debts. In a letter that would not reach his supporters in England for many months, Carey wrote, "I am in a strange land alone, with no Christian friend, a large family, and nothing to supply their wants [needs]."[2] The outlook seemed bleak.

For the next seven years, Carey and his family moved from one location to another as he tried to make ends meet, learn Bengali, translate the New Testament, and preach the gospel to anyone who would listen. Dorothy Carey and her sister, who accompanied the family to India, hated their new life. To make matters worse, Dorothy and their son Peter fell ill with severe dysentery. Peter soon died, and Dorothy began her descent into insanity.

As trial after trial rocked his life, Carey kept his eyes on the goal: "What is there in all this world worth living for, but the presence and service of God? I feel a burning desire that all the world may know this God, and serve Him."[3] Every morning, Carey sought the presence of God. Every day, he strove to serve His Savior.

On January 17, 1794, Carey wrote in his journal:

> Went to Calcutta to Mr. T [Thomas] for money but to no purpose—Was very much dejected all day. Have no relish for anything of the world, yet am swallowed up in its cares— Towards Evening had a pleasant View of the all-sufficiency of God, and the stability of his promises which much relieved my mind—and as I walked home in the Night, was enabled to roll my Soul, and all my Cares in some measure on God; on my coming home I found all much more calm that I expected; for which I bless God—and pray that he may direct us into the patient waiting for Christ.[4]

Despite his abysmal circumstances and lack of key resources, Carey found his sufficiency in God.

In desperation to feed and house his family, Carey moved east of Kolkata and took up farming in Debhatta near the border of modern-day Bangladesh. All the while, his wife's mental condition deteriorated. On April 14, 1794, though struggling with discouragement, Carey again commented in his journal on God's all-sufficiency: "Still a time of Enjoyment of God; I feel that it is good to commit my Soul, my Body, and my All into the hands of God. Then the World appears little, the Promises great, and God an all-sufficient Portion."[5] The next day, despite the tigers that roamed the fields and jungles of Debhatta, Carey ventured outdoors to spend time with God: "Bless God, that His presence is not departed. This evening, during the approach of a violent storm of thunder, I walked alone, and had very sweet converse with God in prayer."[6] The power to plod came from his consistent walk with God.[7]

The farm in Debhatta did not do well, and, in the summer of 1794, Carey moved north to Mudnabati to oversee an indigo plantation. Two years later, Carey's efforts had still produced few spiritual results among the local population. On April 10, 1796, he wrote to his sisters in England:

> I feel as a farmer does about his crop: sometimes I think the seed is springing, and thus I hope; a little blasts all, and my hopes are gone like a cloud. They were only weeds which appeared; or if a little corn sprung up, it quickly dies, being either choked with weeds, or parched up by the sun of persecution. Yet I still hope in God, and will go forth in his strength, and make mention of his righteousness, even of his only [Psalm 71:16].[8]

God empowered Carey to press on.

The barren years would end in late 1799, not long after the arrival of teammates William Ward and Joshua Marshman. However, Carey would never forget what God taught him while he struggled alone those first seven years. By December 1800, Krishna Pal would come to Christ, the first of hundreds of Indians who would convert to Christianity during Carey's lifetime.

Furthermore, Carey's example would revolutionize Christianity's approach to missions. In the decade after the establishment of Carey's Baptist Missionary Society, his work in India would inspire the establishment of no less than five new mission boards in the United Kingdom and the first missionary society in the United States.[9] By obeying the Great Commission and relying on God, Carey launched a gospel movement that would spread around the world.

In times of distress, God is our all-sufficient portion.[10] In his journal, Carey repeatedly claimed this promise as he depended on God. The psalmist Asaph testifies in Psalm 73:26: "My flesh and my heart fail; but God is the strength of my heart and my portion forever." Jeremiah concurs in Lamentations 3:24: "'The Lord is my portion,' says my soul, 'Therefore I hope in Him!'" In the Old Testament, God chose the tribe of Levi to serve Him. Unlike the other eleven tribes, the Levites received no portion of land to cultivate for their livelihood. Instead, the Lord told them, "I am your portion and your inheritance" (Numbers 18:20). God promised to care for Levites as they worked for Him.

Today, when you say the Lord is your portion, you are saying that, even if you lack in other areas, just having God is enough. Trust Him to supply your needs. Look to Him to sustain you through trials. Labor for Him, not for temporal possessions or earthly success. As your all-sufficient portion, God is worthy of your dependence on Him.

PERSONAL REFLECTION

- How willing am I to plod on, depending on God, when times are hard and faithful companions are few?
- What spiritual disciplines do I need to develop so that I am close enough to God to find Him enough when I am lacking important things?
- How can I embrace God as my all-sufficient portion today?

FURTHER READING   Psalm 73:23–28

George, Timothy. *Faithful Witness: The Life and Mission of William Carey*. Birmingham, AL: Christian History Institute, 1998.

NOT GIVING IN WHEN OTHERS GIVE UP

"Our confidence is the strength of the Lord Jesus Christ, whose aid we depend upon, and whose servants we desire to manifest ourselves to be."[1]

—HENRY NOTT, MISSIONARY TO TAHITI (1774–1844)

"At my first defense no one stood with me, but all forsook me. May it not be charged against them. But the Lord stood with me and strengthened me, so that the message might be preached fully through me, and that all the Gentiles might hear. Also I was delivered out of the mouth of the lion."

—2 TIMOTHY 4:16–17

And then there was one. Twenty-four first-time missionaries arrived in Tahiti aboard the *Duff* on March 5, 1797.[2] Just one year later, thirteen deserted the mission, moving to Australia.[3] Not long afterward, two of those remaining in Tahiti apostatized and married idol-worshiping Tahitian women. In 1807, the leader of the team, John Jefferson, passed away.[4] Another teammate went insane, attempting to teach the locals of Tahiti the Hebrew language before falling in love with the queen. Though some reinforcements came, the remaining missionaries abandoned Tahiti for the safety of Australia by the fall of 1809. All left but one. Former bricklayer Henry Nott persevered alone in Tahiti.[5]

The dream to pioneer the gospel in Tahiti began with William Carey. When contemporaries read of Captain James Cook's journeys to the South Pacific, they envisioned adventure or profit, but Carey saw lost souls. However, in July 1793 God led Carey to India instead of Tahiti. Though far from England, Carey's influence for missions continued through his writings, especially his pamphlet *An Inquiry into the Obligation of Christians to Use Means for the Conversion of the Heathen*. When Carey's first missionary letter reached England in July of 1794, a group of pastors in London read it together. Inspired by Carey's work, these pastors united to form the London Missionary Society (LMS).[6] Unsurprisingly, the first field of labor they chose was Tahiti.

However, twelve years after the first LMS missionaries landed in Tahiti, only Henry Nott remained.[7] Nott had been one of the first to finally master enough of the local language to begin preaching from village to village in 1802.[8] Sadly, none of the villagers showed any interest in the gospel. One local said, "You give me much talk and prayers, but very few axes, knives and scissors."[9] As Nott's coworkers had concluded before leaving for Australia, all seemed futile.

A brutal civil war escalated. Pomare, the king of Tahiti, slaughtered dissidents, allowed human sacrifice to continue, and modeled a lifestyle of flagrant immorality. Three times the young queen gave birth only to murder her babies because their fathers had been men of lower class. Then, in what was believed to be a botched abortion, the queen died at age twenty-four.[10] Against such a society, the gospel made no perceivable headway.

Nott looked up beyond the towering mountains of Tahiti to the Creator and Lord of both the beautiful island and its sin-enslaved inhabitants. Pointing to the peak that the locals called "The Diadem," Nott said, "That mountain is symbolic. It is a prophecy. This island will yet become a diadem of redeemed Tahitian jewels."[11] As his faithful coworker John Jefferson had written before his death in 1807,

> Notwithstanding these things are so, we are not in despair. The work we are engaged in is not ours, but God's: it is ours to use the appointed means, His to bless them. . . . we look forward to a period when we hope to see the Word of God run and be glorified [2 Thessalonians 3:1].[12]

Nothing seemed more unlikely in 1810.

Throughout the Tahitian civil war, Nott alone continued building a relationship with King Pomare. The king's losses in battle shattered his faith in the traditional idolatry of Tahiti. By 1812, Pomare started to show interest in the gospel. With the king's increasing support, Nott continued the work his former team had begun—building his vocabulary, reducing the language to writing, and then translating the Bible.

When the war abated and some of Nott's coworkers straggled back to Tahiti, the tide began to turn. In 1815, Pomare started urging his people to forsake their idols. The Tahitians listened to both the king and Nott.

Finally, one local man named Patii promised to destroy his idols. Nott told him, "I can scarcely allow myself to believe what you say." Patii smiled: "Don't be unbelieving; wait till tomorrow and you shall see."[13] The next day, Patii burned his idols in the same place where humans had traditionally been sacrificed.

In 1816, the king mailed his personal idols to the office of the London Missionary Society. Then, on May 16, 1819, Pomare publicly followed Jesus Christ in baptism. However, by that time, hundreds of his subjects had already come to Christ.[14] Over four thousand attended the special worship services coinciding with the king's baptism. Churches sprang up across Tahiti and the surrounding islands.

After nearly twenty years with no visible results, the work of God began to flourish in Tahiti. The debauchery that had threatened the existence of the Tahitian people diminished as the gospel changed lives. In 1816, Tati, a chief who came to Christ, testified: "If God had not sent His word at the time He did, wars, infant murder, human sacrifices, and disease would have made an end of the small remnant of the nation."[15] The gospel not only transformed individuals but also influenced the society of the island.

How did Henry Nott find strength to persevere when everyone else gave up? He kept his eyes on the Lord from the very beginning. When the first wave of missionaries abandoned Tahiti just a year after their arrival, Nott and the few remaining men wrote, "Our confidence is the strength of the Lord Jesus Christ, whose aid we depend upon, and whose servants we desire to manifest ourselves to be."[16] This mindset of dependence on God kept Nott true to God's call when others abandoned the work.

In missions, attrition is a recurring problem. Many new missionary recruits head to the field only to return to their homeland a few years later. Some leave because of factors beyond their control—government policies, illness, or even death. However, many others leave due to issues like wrong expectations, lack of preparation, spiritual immaturity, and conflict with coworkers. Only dependence on Christ can sustain and grow God's servants in such circumstances.

In local churches across the world, believers also retreat from passionate service for Jesus. What begins at conversion as white-hot enthusiasm for God and His work often cools over time into duty-driven complacency. When difficulties arise or seemingly more attractive opportunities present themselves, these lukewarm believers begin to fill their time with other priorities.

What is the antidote for spiritual apathy and missionary attrition? Jesus Himself gave the answer in Revelation 3:20. Speaking to believers, He warns of divine discipline for lukewarmness and invites us to draw close to Him: "Behold, I stand at the door and knock. If anyone hears My voice and opens the door, I will come in to him and dine with him, and he with Me." Strength to persevere comes from fellowship with Christ. Draw near to Him. Only time alone with Jesus can rekindle your zeal and keep you from giving in when those around you are giving up.

PERSONAL REFLECTION

- When others turn back from serving God, what will keep me faithful to God's calling in my life?
- In what ways have I become lukewarm toward God and His work?
- To what extent is my desire for success in serving God greater than my dedication to faithfully follow God's leading no matter what the results?

FURTHER READING   Revelation 3:14–22

DAY 3

NOT INDISPENSABLE

"I was beginning to look upon myself as somewhat indispensable. So the Lord had to teach me that I was not. . . . It is great to sit at the Master's feet and learn of Him!"

—ERNIE PRESSWOOD, MISSIONARY TO INDONESIA (1908–1946)

"Always in every prayer of mine making request for you all with joy, for your fellowship in the gospel from the first day until now, being confident of this very thing, that He who has begun a good work in you will complete it until the day of Jesus Christ."

—PHILIPPIANS 1:4–6

"What is this?" Dyak villager Panai Raub asked himself as he entered a clearing deep in the jungles of Indonesia's island of Borneo (modern-day Kalimantan). A tall foreigner stood with eyes closed and arms outstretched. Surrounding him were scores of Dyaks, heads bowed. Raub, like many Dyaks in the early 1930s, had stumbled upon his first contact with Christians, and they were all praying.

Then, the foreigner—twenty-four-year-old Canadian Ernie Presswood—preached the gospel. Presswood wrote of his early experiences:

> As far as I know, there is not one soul here who knows what it is to be saved. . . . For many centuries these people have been under the bondage and fear of Satan. The fruits he has produced greatly resemble himself: ignorance, superstition, witchcraft, corruption of mind, filth, disease and suffering—these follow in the path of the prince of the power of the air. Only the firm hand of the Dutch [colonial government] keeps the villagers from indulging in the old orgies of headhunting and tribal warfare. . . . Nevertheless, we feel the Sun of Righteousness is about to rise above this dark picture with healing in His wings [Malachi 4:2].[1]

Presswood was right, and God would use him to spark the transformation.

As local villagers turned to Christ, the Dyaks began calling Presswood "Tuan Change," meaning "Mr. Change." The gospel transformed those who believed into new creations in Christ. Presswood reported how God had unusually worked among the Dyaks: "Everywhere crowds gathered and followed from village to village. . . . There is no explanation for this except that in answer to the prayers of God's people."[2] God used Presswood to launch the initial movement, but as the gospel momentum increased, He moved others to further the work. Panai Raub and other local leaders not only believed the gospel but also caught Presswood's passion for its spread. With neither urging nor organizing by the foreigners, these local men took the message to surrounding villages where the missionaries could not go.[3]

Although this fruitful season was just beginning, God removed Presswood as the point man for the advance. An ulcer in his foot forced him from the jungles of Borneo back to his mission headquarters in Makassar, Celebes (modern-day Ujung Pandung, Sulewesi). Surgery required seven months of recovery. He wrote of this time:

> Because [God] sees our need, even though we fail to, He brings us through all sorts of trials and testings that we may come and learn of Him. Like Martha of old, I was "cumbered about much serving" [Luke 10:38–42]. I was beginning to look upon myself as somewhat indispensable. So the Lord had to teach me that I was not. . . . It is great to sit at the Master's feet and learn of Him! I have learned some things that I ought to have learned long ago. . . . The work we are engaged in is His. He will clearly reveal each step we should take and supply every need. [4]

God did just that, leading Presswood back to the growing work in Borneo when his foot finally healed.

After over seven years in the jungles, Presswood returned to Makassar in 1941. There, he led a Bible institute for training local pastors for the churches that had sprung up in the jungles of Indonesia. His new wife, Ruth, a nurse fresh from the United States, joined him. [5]

However, in 1942 God interrupted Presswood's labors once again—this time for three years in a Japanese internment camp during World War II. [6] Often confined in shelters built for pigs and forced to labor like slaves, Presswood and his coworker, Russell Deibler, served where God placed them. As men died of disease in the torrid tropical climate, Presswood and Deibler shared the gospel, encouraged the weak, and comforted the bereaved with the promises of God's Word. Yet, Presswood kept his eyes on the goal. A fellow prisoner noted that "Presswood earnestly prepared himself for his task after the war. . . . How often had he prayed to be free again, to be able to work for Christ!"[7] Once the Australians liberated Sulewesi, Presswood hit the ground running.

By November 27, 1945, Presswood and his wife had returned to Borneo.[8] He discovered that, despite the war, the Dyak church had continued to grow and spread. One European observer noted that Dyaks spent approximately one-third of the year intoxicated, but where the gospel went, that number plummeted dramatically.[9] The violence, too, decreased. The administrator of a neighboring region told Presswood, "Your Dyaks are different," and he asked for Christian Dyak teachers to be sent to his region.[10]

Though Presswood had already began to push forward, God once again interrupted his plans—this time permanently. The privations of the internment camp had taken their toll. After a trek deep into the jungle, Presswood's body succumbed to a fever that he would probably have survived before the war.

Presswood's work came to a close, but God's work did not.[11] As the apostle Paul said in Philippians 1:6, "He who has begun a good work in you will complete it until the day of Jesus Christ." This promise is true both in the spiritual lives of individuals as well as the overall growth of God's church. In the following decade, the gospel would continue its spread across Borneo.

Serve faithfully. Wrestle in prayer. Depend on God's strength. Dodge the lie of your own indispensability. Do not fear when factors beyond your control sideline you. Seize these times of divine interruption as opportunities to rest at the Master's feet. As Presswood learned early on, "the work we are engaged in is His." When your role is finished, God will further His own work.

PERSONAL REFLECTION

- How has God temporarily interrupted my life so that I can learn to rely on Him more?
- What is my typical response when circumstances beyond my control keep me from doing what I have a passion to do? How might God want me to grow in my response to these obstacles?
- How can I increase the ratio of time I spend "at Jesus' feet" in relation to time "cumbered about much serving"?

FURTHER READING   Luke 10:38–42

Hutchins, Ruth Presswood. *No Sacrifice Too Great.* Chicago: Moody Publishers, 1993.

OPPORTUNITY IN THE IMPOSSIBLE

"May it not be that the human impossibility is just the very thing that sets His hand free?"

—LILIAS TROTTER, MISSIONARY TO ALGERIA (1853–1928)

"If you have faith as a mustard seed, you will say to this mountain, 'Move from here to there,' and it will move; and nothing will be impossible for you."

—MATTHEW 17:20

They are sorceresses," the locals murmured as Lilias Trotter and Blanche Haworth trudged into a village high in the mountains above the desert city of Biskra, Algeria. In mid-February 1902, two single British women in their late forties led a couple of mules laden with Bibles and tracts for distribution. For centuries, the gospel had rarely, if ever, reached this far into the northern edge of the Sahara.

Bedraggled from torrential downpours along the dirt trail and an unfortunate slip into a watering hole, the women may have initially suspected that their appearance caused the locals to shy away from them. However, Trotter and Haworth soon learned the truth: the French colonial government had sent word ahead. No one wanted to be fined or jailed for associating with the "sorceresses" or accepting their literature.

Trotter spotted two familiar French faces in the crowd of locals.

"Bonjour!" She grinned at the spies for the colonial government that had followed the women each step of their journey. At times, the French officials hindered their ability to buy supplies, but the women persevered.[1] Though the work in Algeria often seemed impossible, Trotter had learned to attempt the impossible in the Lord's strength.

Saved at a young age, Trotter grew up in a wealthy Christian home with many spiritual influences. As a teenager, she attended an influential conference on sanctification and spiritual life.[2] Then, when American evangelist D. L. Moody traveled to Britain on an evangelistic campaign, twenty-two-year-old Trotter attended his training sessions and served as a counselor, leading people to Christ after the evangelist's sermons.[3] With the launch of the Young Women's Christian Association, Trotter's service to Christ expanded.[4] Those in Trotter's aristocratic class were expected to do social service, but this focused young woman took her ministries to a level that astonished her peers.

In May 1887, Trotter heard a missionary to northern Africa tell of the spiritual plight of the Arab world. He spoke on a Thursday night and mentioned that just the previous Sunday he had preached in Algeria. Trotter knew that the needs of London were great, but if she could travel to Algeria in just half a week, why not serve there? The spiritual needs of northern Africa far outweighed those of England where many Christians could take her place!

Trotter applied to the North Africa Mission. Despite her passion for the Lord's work, the mission declined her application due to concerns about her medical evaluation. Undaunted, she struck an agreement with the mission to work alongside but not under them.[5] As a well-off aristocrat, Trotter could support herself whether in England or in Algeria. She would bear responsibility for the health risks she would encounter abroad.

Trotter would serve in Algeria for the next forty years. She and a growing band of coworkers would establish a ministry headquarters to reach Muslim women in the Arab section of the city of Algiers.[6] When possible, she would head south toward the Sahara, hauling as many Bibles and books as her camels or mules could carry. The Wordless Book was often her tool for sharing the gospel.[7]

Cultural, religious, and governmental opposition often slowed the pioneer work to a crawl. In 1895, Trotter wrote, "There are times when . . . human hope and courage flag—and only the . . . 'faith of the Son of God' can overleap [sic] the difficulties and discouragements and land down with both feet on the promises of God."[8] Pondering similar difficulties a few years later, she wrote in her diary: "The things that are impossible with men are possible with God. May it not be that the human impossibility is just the very thing that sets His Hand Free?"[9] In a 1901 entry, she continued on the same theme:

> I am seeing more & more that we begin to learn what it is to
> walk by faith, when we learn to spread out all there is against
> us. All our physical weakness—loss of mental power—spiritual

inability—all that is against us inwardly & outwardly, as sails to the wind & expect them to be vehicles for the power of Christ to rest upon us.[10]

In 1905, she would similarly write: "It is only beyond what is humanly reasonable & possible that we see the Glory of God."[11] Though the work among the Muslims was hard and the results were few, Trotter firmly believed that the impossibility itself was the arena for God to work.[12]

Compounding the difficulties of ministry in Algeria, Trotter's health often slowed her ministry. Following a medical crisis in 1895, she learned that because of her weakened heart she must pace herself year-round. Most importantly, in an era without air conditioning, she must escape the equatorial heat of summer, resting in Switzerland or England. Her intense nature often balked at the necessity for these convalescent retreats.

Never one to waste time, Trotter would use these periods of forced seclusion to commune with God, to write, and to paint. In August 1899, she sought an evergreen forest where she could spend "one week alone with God."[13] Exactly one year later, she ventured out on the heathered moors of England. From there, she wrote, "Oh so endlessly beautiful the days are—& they go so quickly—God has many things to say & one can sit by the hour on the heather with one's Bible and listen."[14] The delays that obstructed her work became a source of spiritual strength for life and ministry.[15]

As she gained experience in the work and depth in her spiritual walk, God increasingly opened opportunities for writing, especially during the periods of waiting. She dedicated her first work, *Parables of the Cross*, to missionary Amy Carmichael with whom she corresponded in India.[16] In addition, Trotter got to know Dr. Samuel Zwemer, a younger missionary in Cairo, who published many of her works through his Nile Mission Press.[17] Her handwritten, illustrated pamphlets appealed to her Arab audience and spread across northern Africa. One quote from an English devotional, titled *Focused*, has endured well beyond her lifetime. Trotter wrote, "Turn full your soul's vision to Jesus, and look at Him, and a strange dimness will come over all that is apart from Him." These words inspired the poet Helen Howarth Lemmel to compose the hymn, "Turn Your Eyes Upon Jesus."[18] What Trotter had learned of dependence on Jesus from years of faithful service became an encouragement to generations of Christians that would sing the biblical truths that she shared.

When you face what seems impossible, turn your eyes upon Jesus. View human impossibility as the opportunity for God to work. Depend on Jesus, remembering His promise in Matthew 17:20 that "nothing will be impossible" to those who trust Him. When your resources are obviously inadequate and your strength undeniably spent, God's power shines with brightness heightened by the dim shadows of human impossibility.

PERSONAL REFLECTION

- If something God wants me to do seems impossible, do I see this as a reason to give up or as an opportunity for God to show Himself strong?
- How can I turn the physical limitations in my life into something with value?
- When do I turn my eyes upon Jesus—is it only when I come to the end of myself or is it at the very outset of every day?

FURTHER READING   John 11:1–44

Rockness, Miriam Huffman. *A Passion for the Impossible: The Life of Lilias Trotter*. Grand Rapids, MI: Discovery House, 2003.

STRENGTH FOR THE BLUE TIMES

"Unprayed for, I feel very much as if a diver were sent down to the bottom of a river with no air to breathe, or as if a fireman were sent up to a blazing building and held an empty hose."
—JAMES GILMOUR, MISSIONARY TO MONGOLIA AND CHINA
(1843–1891)

"When you pass through the waters, I will be with you."
—ISAIAH 43:2

Mongolian and Chinese alike stared at James Gilmour. The young Brit was riding his donkey backwards. For once, a companion—Joseph Edkins—had joined him on one of his missionary journeys. In the summer of 1872, the two men traveled two hundred miles from Beijing to Wu Tai Shan, a mountaintop gathering place for Mongolians in the northern Chinese province of Shanxi. Gilmour seized the opportunity for fellowship—except the donkeys would not cooperate. The beasts insisted on walking single file no matter how wide the road was. So Gilmour took the lead, and facing the tail of his donkey, he conversed with his coworker who rode properly on the following donkey.[1]

Although Edkins accompanied Gilmour on this particular trip within China, nobody wanted to join him long-term in Mongolia. He begged the London Missionary Society for a partner, but no one volunteered. The intense cold and darkness of the Mongolian winters did nothing to help with recruitment. The necessity of constant travel to reach the nomadic locals further limited the potential candidates. Gilmour was alone.

Originally, the opportunity to launch out on his own had excited Gilmour. His first exploratory trip into the frozen north convinced him otherwise. His loneliness, exacerbated by his ignorance of Chinese, Russian, and Mongolian, drove his mind to dark places. On September 18, 1870, he wrote,

> Today I felt a good deal like Elijah in the wilderness. He prayed that he might die. I wonder if I am telling the truth when I say that I felt drawn towards suicide. I take this opportunity of declaring strongly that on all occasions two missionaries should go together. I was not of this opinion a few weeks ago, but I had no idea how weak an individual I am. My eyes have filled with tears frequently these last few days in spite of myself. Oh! The intense loneliness of Christ's life, not a single one understood Him! He bore it. O Jesus, let me follow in thy steps![2]

After four years of traveling alone across Mongolia, still no one would come, but God had not forgotten Gilmour. Instead of sending Gilmour a coworker, God provided him a wife.[3]

Beginning in late 1874, Emily Gilmour joined her husband on his itinerant, evangelistic journeys. Beijing served as their headquarters. From there, the intrepid couple hauled their blue tent across the deserts and mountains of Mongolia. During the bitterest winter weather, they joined in the outreaches to the Chinese in Beijing and made contact with Mongolians who also wintered in the Chinese capital city. Gilmour's spirits rose, even though the success of their Mongolian work did not.

More than ever, Gilmour recognized his need for prayer. In 1882, Gilmour and his wife returned to Britain for their first furlough. Speaking to supporters, he emphasized the vital role of prayer for their isolated Mongolian mission:

> Unprayed for, I feel very much as if a diver were sent down to the bottom of a river with no air to breathe, or as if a fireman were sent up to a blazing building and held an empty hose; I feel very much as a soldier who is firing blank cartridge at an enemy, and so I ask you earnestly to pray that the Gospel may take saving and working effect on the minds of those men to whose notice it has been introduced by us.[4]

Gilmour knew that only God could change the hearts of the Mongolians, most of whom did not "care one straw for Christianity."[5]

In addition to his pleas for the intercession of others, Gilmour also prioritized personal prayer.[6] In his journal entry for October 14, 1871, Gilmour records a typical start to his day: "To-day rose before the sun, read [Mongolian] words, wrote at the account of my journey from Urga, went to the mountain for devotion."[7] In some areas, Gilmour's treks into the wilderness to be alone with God would arouse the suspicions of the local Mongolians, so Gilmour had no choice but stay in his tent to read and pray, regardless of whoever wandered in. He noted, "At our meals, our devotions, our ablutions [washing up], there they were—much amused and interested."[8] In time, the young couple adapted to the interruptions and continued their time with God.

On September 19, 1885, after nearly eleven years of marriage, Emily Gilmour died of a lung disease, and Gilmour went on without a companion. He left Beijing and moved to the more settled, agricultural area of eastern Mongolia. He traveled between three villages, staying in rustic inns and sharing the gospel with individuals. He saw very little fruit, and his spirits sunk once again.

Prolonged periods of loneliness led to feelings of despondency, yet he kept on. His journals often marked his down times with words like, "felt blue today." Sometimes, these "blue" periods would last several days. However, God sent rays of hope into the darkness. For example, he wrote,

> In August [1886] we again visited Ta Cheng Tzu. I was blue. The fever of July, the defection of the Mongol donkey man, who failed to come for us, the diarrhoea [sic] which on the journey changed to dysentery, being baffled in attempting to find suitable quarters in Ta Cheng Tzu, and the chilled hearts of the restaurant men [as a result of the poor testimony of a foreign Christian], made our entrance not cheerful. On the way my assistant and I had talked over matters, and resolved by prayer and endeavour to see what could be done for the restaurant men. Just ten days after our arrival the eldest brother called on me in my inn and said, "To-night I dismiss my gods, henceforth I am a Christian. I am ready to be baptized any day you may be pleased to name."[9]

Gilmour wrote of his relief and joy because of this man's unexpected conversion to Christ and zeal for sharing his new faith with those in the restaurant. However, triumphs like this were few and far between. As he plodded on, Gilmour begged his mission to send him a coworker.

Finally, on March 24, 1888, the London Missionary Society sent Gilmour a partner, a medical doctor named Roberts. But just one month after his arrival, Roberts transferred to a new post. The head doctor at the mission hospital in the port city of Tianjin unexpectedly passed away, and the mission recalled Roberts to take his place. Gilmour reeled at the news.[10]

Once again, Gilmour soldiered on alone. He wrote,

> My faith is not gone, but it would be untrue to say that I am not walking in the dark. I shall do my best to hold on here single-handed; but I earnestly hope that I am not to be alone much longer. Something must be done. There is a limit to all human endurance.[11]

About a year later in March 1889, another physician, Dr. Smith, joined him. Upon seeing Gilmour's physical and emotional deterioration, this doctor's first act was to send Gilmour back to England for rest. Gilmour returned to Mongolia eight months later, fully recovered and ready to press on once again.

How was Gilmour able to persevere without family or coworkers? How did he stave off deep discouragement in a land of spiritual hardness, soul-killing darkness, life-disrupting disease, and extreme cold? What sustained his faith when the Mongolians—with very few exceptions—showed no interest in Christ? His own prayer life, the prayers of God's people for him, and the promises of God's Word enabled him to remain faithful to the Lord.

Just over a year after his wife's death, Gilmour sat alone in his tent, desperately in need of companionship. He wrote in his journal: "I am reading at night, before going to bed, the Psalms . . . and

I find much strength and courage in the old warrior's words. Verily, the Psalms are inspired. No doubt about that. None that wait on Him will be put to shame [Psalm 25:3]. He is here with me." [12] Only a vibrant relationship with God based on the promises of God's Word and braced by a fervent prayer life can sustain God's people when bereaved and abandoned in a dark, cold world.

God never promises an easy life. "Blue times" of prolonged disappointment and even despondency may dog your path. However, God assures His people that no matter where He leads, He is with you: "Yea, though I walk through the valley of the shadow of death, I will fear no evil; For You are with me" (Psalm 23:4). When no one will join you or those once with you are gone, God is still there. He promises, "When you pass through the waters, I will be with you" (Isaiah 43:2). Like Gilmour, look to God's Word for hope: "To You, O Lord, I lift up my soul. O my God, I trust in You; Let me not be ashamed; Let not my enemies triumph over me. Indeed, let no one who waits on You be ashamed" (Psalm 25:1–3). Wait on God and soldier on with Him.

PERSONAL REFLECTION

- Is my spiritual walk with God fervent enough to sustain me if I were isolated from all other Christians?
- Where do I turn when facing dark thoughts or unrelenting discouragement?
- How often do I pray for and encourage missionaries who live far from their homeland in difficult regions of the world?

FURTHER READING   1 Kings 19:9–21

Lovett, Richard. *James Gilmour of Mongolia: His Diaries, Letters, and Reports*. London: Religious Tract Society, 1895.

Gilmour, James. *Among the Mongols*. London: Religious Tract Society, 1883.

DAY 6

ONLY ONE LIFE

"Oh let my love with fervor burn,
And from the world now let me turn;
Living for Thee, and Thee alone,
Bringing Thee pleasure on Thy throne;
Only one life, 'twill soon be past,
Only what's done for Christ will last."

—C. T. STUDD, MISSIONARY TO CHINA, INDIA, AND THE CONGO
(1860–1931)

"One thing I do, forgetting those things which are behind and
reaching forward to those things which are ahead, I press
toward the goal for the prize of the upward call of God in
Christ Jesus."

—PHILIPPIANS 3:13–14

Crack!" With a mighty swing, twenty-two-year-old C. T. Studd struck the ball. Spindly chairs tipped to the grass as the crowd rose to cheer their star. With Studd on the squad, the Cambridge University cricket team's chances of victory skyrocketed. In 1882, Studd led them to defeat Australia, setting records along the way. No one played cricket the way Studd did. His enthusiasm and focus outshone both competitors and teammates alike. But little did he know, a new passion would soon replace his love for athletics.

Studd grew up in a wealthy, nominally Christian home. During D. L. Moody's 1877 evangelistic campaigns in Britain, Studd's father was born again. He urged his three teenage sons who were students at a boarding school in Eton to believe. On the same day, all three trusted Christ as Savior.

However, C. T. soon backslid to his former habits, prioritizing sports over his walk with God. Studd wrote of this time: "I was selfish and kept the knowledge [of Christ] to myself. Gradually my love began to grow cold, and the love of the world began to come in. I spent six years in that unhappy backslidden state."[1] But God would get his attention.

In 1884, Studd's brother George became deathly ill. As Studd sat beside his brother's bed, the Lord worked in the young cricketer's heart. Studd asked himself, "Now what is all the world's popularity worth to George? What are fame and flattery worth? Is it worth possessing all the world's riches, when a man faces eternity?" The words of Solomon echoed in his mind: "Vanity of vanities, all is vanity [Ecclesiastes 1:2]."[2] Though his brother recovered from his illness, Studd was never the same.

The young man threw himself into evangelistic work with the same passion he had devoted to playing cricket. He joined Moody's campaigns and learned to share the gospel.[3] When Studd led a man to Christ for salvation, the experience greatly moved him. He wrote, "I cannot tell you what joy it gave me to bring the first soul to the Lord Jesus Christ. I have tasted almost all the pleasures this world can give. I do not suppose there is one I have not experienced, but I can tell you that those pleasures were as nothing compared to the joy the saving of that one soul gave me."[4] When cricket season began, Studd had a new goal. He wrote,

> "[I] must go into the cricket field and get the men there to know the Lord Jesus. Formerly I had as much love for cricket as a man could have, but . . . I found that I had something infinitely better than cricket. My heart was no longer in the game; I wanted to win souls for the Lord. I knew that cricket would not last, and honor would not last, and nothing in this world would last, but it was worth while [sic] living for the world to come."[5]

Studd had not yet written his famous poem, but the idea was born in these early days: "Only one life, 'twill soon be past, / Only what's done for Christ will last."

Studd packed enough into his one life to fill the lives of three men. He would soon trade the cricket field for the mission field. He first served in China for fifteen years before health problems forced him and his family back to England. After he recovered, Studd followed God's leading to India for six years.[6] Once again Studd's health failed, and he returned to the West. During this time, the veteran missionary lent his voice to the budding Student Volunteer Movement in Britain and the United States that urged Christian youths to serve in missions overseas.

In 1908, the spiritual needs of central Africa lit a new fire in Studd's heart. Friends, doctors, and even his wife pleaded with him not to go. Nearing fifty years old with a history of asthma and recurring malaria, Studd's chances of survival in Africa did not look good. However, Studd stubbornly refused to listen to any advice: "God has called me to go, and I will go. I will blaze the trail, though my grave may only become a stepping stone that younger men may follow."[7] True to his word, Studd left for the Belgian Congo (modern-day Democratic Republic of the Congo) alone on December 15, 1910. For the last twenty years of his life, Studd blazed that trail, establishing the Heart of Africa Mission and bringing the light of the gospel to thousands who had never heard.[8] Though health problems had forced him to relinquish his work in China and India, Studd let nothing persuade him to leave the interior of Africa.

The longer he lived, the more Studd's passion compelled him to press on. At times, especially later in life, that intensity drove people away from him and created controversy. However, he always pushed forward.[9]

What fueled Studd's passion? What sustained him despite physical weakness? A major factor was his time alone with God.

Beginning early in his ministry, Studd prioritized his walk with God. Writing from Pingyang, China, on February 7, 1886, he describes his devotions in his characteristically flamboyant manner:

> The Lord is so good and always gives a large dose of Spiritual Champagne every morning which braces one up for the day and night. Of late I have had such glorious times. I generally wake about 3:30 a.m. and feel quite wide awake, so have a good read, etc. And then have an hour's sleep or so before finally getting up. I find what I read then is stamped indelibly on my mind all through the day.[10]

A habit like that can permanently mark a life and fuel it with passion for God and His work.[11]

Studd not only modeled dedication to Christ, but he also expressed it through his publications for his mission, an essay in *The Fundamentals*, and even poetry. His famous "two little lines" grace plaques in churches and homes across the world. Few today realize these lines are part of a longer poem—a poem well worth reading as a fitting conclusion to this snapshot of one driven servant of God.

> Two little lines I heard one day,
> Traveling along life's busy way;
> Bringing conviction to my heart,
> And from my mind would not depart;
> Only one life, 'twill soon be past,
> Only what's done for Christ will last.
>
> Only one life, yes only one,
> Soon will its fleeting hours be done;
> Then, in 'that day' my Lord to meet,
> And stand before His Judgment seat;
> Only one life, 'twill soon be past,
> Only what's done for Christ will last.
>
> Only one life, a few brief years,
> Each with its burdens, hopes, and fears;
> Each with its days I must fulfill,
> Living for self or in His will;
> Only one life, 'twill soon be past,
> Only what's done for Christ will last.
>
> When this bright world would tempt me sore,
> When Satan would a victory score;
> When self would seek to have its way,
> Then help me Lord with joy to say;

Only one life, 'twill soon be past,
Only what's done for Christ will last.

Give me Father, a purpose deep,
In joy or sorrow Thy word to keep;
Faithful and true what e'er the strife,
Pleasing Thee in my daily life;
Only one life, 'twill soon be past,
Only what's done for Christ will last.

Only one life, yes only one,
Now let me say, "Thy will be done";
And when at last I'll hear the call,
I know I'll say, "'Twas worth it all";
Only one life, 'twill soon be past,
Only what's done for Christ will last.[12]

PERSONAL REFLECTION

- How am I spending my one life? What time is routinely being wasted?
- Do I think it is possible to be too passionate for God and His work? Why or why not?
- What am I unwilling to give up for Christ?

FURTHER READING   2 Timothy 4:1–8

Pollock, John. *The Cambridge Seven.* Fearn, Ross-shire, Scotland: Christian Focus Publications, 2006.

DAY 7

EXTREME UNCERTAINTY

"We felt so alone—but alone with God!" [1]
—JEAN DYE JOHNSON, MISSIONARY TO BOLIVIA (1920–2012)

"Yet I will rejoice in the Lord,
I will joy in the God of my salvation.
The Lord God is my strength."
—HABAKKUK 3:18-19

I f you don't hear anything inside a month, you can come and make a search for us." [2] With those words, Cecil Dye led his brother Bob and three missionary coworkers into the jungles known as Bolivia's Green Hell. One month later with no word from the expedition, Jean Dye, Bob's young wife, hoped against hope for their return.

In May 1943 in the thick of World War II and less than seven months before the five men vanished into the jungle, Jean had arrived in Bolivia. She journeyed to the remote region that formed an indistinct panhandle between Brazil and Paraguay. Less than a month later, she married Bob Dye. The whole time, Jean knew the risks.

As the first missionary team of the fledgling New Tribes Mission (known today as Ethnos360), they had come to spread the gospel to the Ayoré people. This nomadic tribe lived isolated in the dense jungle. The nearby Bolivians called them *bárbaros*, meaning savages. Jean's new brother-in-law, Cecil Dye, was one of the founders of New Tribes Mission and the leader of the expedition. As they formulated their plans, the team dedicated two weeks to prayer. Then, they spent months hacking with machetes through virgin jungle to reach the Sansa Hills where the Ayoré roamed. On November 10, 1943, the jungle swallowed the five men.

Married for less than six months, Jean Dye confronted the reality that she might be a widow. Yet, for the next four years, she and the two other missionary wives remained in limbo, unsure of the fate of their husbands. When rescue missions returned with no definite answers, the women prayed, waited, and hoped. Maybe the five men had been captured. Maybe they would just reappear one day out of the jungle. Maybe the women really were widows.

Jean struggled. The other ladies had children. Jean had nothing tangible left of her young husband. For months after Bob's disappearance, she hid her inner turmoil, but finally, she dissolved into tears. Jean wrote what God taught her through her sorrow:

> "My grief is selfish! My tears are tears of self-pity!" The word self-pity seared me as deeply as the word indulge [indulge in tears]. At last I saw my problem. God did not want me to pine my life away feeling sorry for myself. My only solution lay in a renewed dedication to Him. "Lord, I believe You are able to keep Bob and to use him, if he's still alive." I affirmed my faith in God

to this end. "But if he's already up there in Heaven with You, then I dedicate myself to do the work of both of us. You will help me!"[3]

The uncertainty of her circumstances had not changed, but Jean's perspective had.

As the spring flowers of 1944 blossomed, Jean threw herself wholeheartedly into the mission that both she and her husband had come to further. More than ever, she desired to reach the Ayoré with the gospel. However, contact with the tribe was rare and remained perilous. In the meantime, Jean taught her coworkers' children, while taking every opportunity to learn the Ayoré language. She spent hours with two Ayoré servants who had been captured by local ranchers and assimilated into local Bolivian culture. In a letter to friends in the U.S., Jean explained her situation: "There's no more news of our loved ones.... It's our business now to settle down to the work at hand.... God has taught us lesson after lesson till we learned not even to wonder about the future, but to leave it in His hands."[4] Jean's faith in God's sovereignty sustained her.

In 1947, Jean and her coworkers developed meaningful contact with a group of Ayoré, far south from where the five men had disappeared.[5] By mid-1948, many Ayoré families had given up their fearsome ways and established their own village, not far from the town of San Juan. Jean helped communicate with the Ayoré until the team was able to share the gospel with them. Still, Jean had no direct confirmation regarding her husband's fate.

However, God answered her prayers for the genuine conversion of men and women from this unreached people group. Jean listened as an Ayoré believer named Degui thanked the Lord for the salvation of his spouse: "Our Father God, thank You for making my wife good." The former warrior continued praying for those who had not yet received Christ's righteousness by faith: "Dupade [God], make them believe You and help me to tell them Your Words."[6] The new believers did not just pray about reaching their countrymen with the gospel. Some left their new village to evangelize their relatives to the north. Others from the north began visiting the new Ayoré town in the south.

Soon, Jean and her coworkers met eyewitnesses to the fate of the five missing missionaries. They learned that a dispute over the gifts the missionaries had brought to encourage friendship had led to their murder. Bob Dye, his brother Cecil Dye, Dave Bacon, George Hosbach, and Eldon Hunter had given their lives to take the gospel to the Ayoré people.

The four years of uncertainty ended in grief but also relief as these families finally knew what had occurred. Jean came to view her husband and his four companions as five seeds that God had planted. As Tertullian wrote during Roman times, "The blood of the martyrs is the seed of the church." Through the sacrifice of these five men, a church of born-again Ayoré men and women emerged out of tragedy.

The new Ayoré believers marveled at the forgiveness of the three widows. Degui prayed, "Thank You that Wana [Jean's Ayoré name] has come back to us. Thank You that she isn't angry with us for having killed her husband."[7] What a testimony to God's grace and transforming power.

The nearby non-Christian Bolivians also could not believe the change in the people they considered to be bárbaros. In one gathering, an Ayoré believer named Ecarai addressed his new neighbors: "Here I am . . . an Ayoré that has come from the jungles to tell you people who are civilized about Jesus Christ."[8] The once unreached tribe now reached out.

Why was Jean Dye—a young widow far from home and family—able to persevere in the face of such tragedy and loss? Where did she find her strength during four years of extreme uncertainty? Jean rested in God's hands, dedicated herself to serve others, and spent daily time with God.[9]

Like Jean Dye, the prophet Habakkuk faced uncertainty in the days leading up to the Babylonian captivity. God warned him that famine, war, destruction, and death would come to his beloved homeland. Life as he knew it would end. Overwhelmed with grief, Habakkuk expressed his feelings in poetry: "When I heard, my body trembled; my lips quivered at the voice; rottenness entered my bones; and I trembled in myself" (Habakkuk 3:16). Despite his weakness and discouragement, the prophet chose to live by faith (Habakkuk 2:4). He purposed to continue serving God, writing, "Yet I will rejoice in the Lord, I will joy in the God of my salvation. The Lord God is my strength" (Habakkuk 3:18–19).

Strength in the face of tragedy comes only through your walk with God. When those closest to you are no longer there, cling to the one relationship that cannot be broken—your relationship with God. As Jean testified, "We felt so alone—but alone with God!"[10]

PERSONAL REFLECTION

- Where is my focus when I suffer loss? Is it more on my loss than it is on Jesus?
- When I feel alone, to what or to whom do I often turn instead of God?
- How much loss am I willing to risk to follow God's leading and make a difference for Him in this world?

FURTHER READING   Habakkuk 3:16–19

Johnson, Jean Dye. *God Planted Five Seeds.* Sanford, FL: Ethnos360, 1966.

SOAKING
BEFORE GOD

"If this time of soaking before God is being spent
in getting rooted and grounded in God . . . ,
you will remain true to Him whatever happens."[1]

—OSWALD CHAMBERS, VOLUNTEER WWI CHAPLAIN IN EGYPT
(1874–1917)

"Draw near to God, and He will draw near to you."

—JAMES 4:8

O swald Chambers pulled back the door flap of his tent and gazed into the Egyptian desert. The first rays of daylight blazed over the sand. At 6:00 a.m. in October 1916, forty-two-year-old Chambers readied himself for the stifling heat and exhausting work ahead. Hundreds of soldiers would cross his path that day as he served as a volunteer YMCA chaplain during World War I.[2]

As the dry desert wind rippled the canvas of his tent, Chambers pored over the open Bible in his lap. On a small table nearby lay his prayer list, prayer journal, and *Daily Light*, a small devotional book of topical Bible readings. The sunrise illuminated his time of meditation on God.

Chambers enjoyed spending time with God in nature. As an artistic youth struggling with God's will for his life, he had often wandered the countryside near Dunoon, Scotland. He would climb Ben Nevis, Great Britain's highest mountain, praying alone to God.

Sometimes, Chambers would seek out John Cameron, an elderly Christian mentor. Together, they would hunt rabbits and talk of spiritual things. On one hike in the Scottish Highlands during the summer of 1897, Chambers and Cameron stopped along the trail to pray. However, their collie puppy would have none of it, barking and nipping at them so they could not concentrate on their petitions to God.

"Hoot, hoot," said Cameron in his thick Scottish brogue. "I will sit on the dog while you pray." [3] The old man seized the collie by the scruff of his neck and sat on him.

Early in his life, Chambers developed the habit of seeking his strength from the Lord and relying on the Holy Spirit. This consistent time with God led to his conviction that life should be "Jesus only, Jesus ever." [4] As his walk with God deepened, his teaching did also. God opened doors for ministry, and many flocked to hear him preach. [5]

In 1911 after a few years of itinerant ministry in the United Kingdom, the United States, and Japan, Chambers opened the Bible Training College in London. Though the college only had a few hundred students during its four years of existence, forty alumni went on to serve as missionaries. Noted preachers of the day, including G. Campbell Morgan and C. T. Studd, sometimes served as guest lecturers.

As he trained young men and women, he stressed the importance of the believer's walk with God:

> The great enemy to the Lord Jesus Christ in the present day is
> the conception of practical work that has not come from the
> New Testament, but from the systems of the world in which
> endless energy and activities are insisted upon, but no private
> life with God. It is not its practical activities that are the strength
> of this Bible Training College, its whole strength lies in the
> fact that here you are put into soak before God. You have no
> idea of where God is going to engineer your circumstances,
> no knowledge of what strain is going to be put on you either
> at home or abroad, and if you waste your time in overactive
> energies instead of getting into soak on the great fundamental
> truths of God's Redemption, you will snap when the strain
> comes; but if this time of soaking before God is being spent in
> getting rooted and grounded in God on the unpractical line, you
> will remain true to Him whatever happens.[6]

Chambers spoke from past experience, but he would need to lean on these lessons again.

In 1914, World War I shattered the world as Chambers and his generation knew it. One year later, Chambers closed the Bible Training College to serve as a volunteer chaplain for Allied troops fighting in northern Africa and the Middle East. Disillusioned soldiers crowded his tent meetings in the desert. Knowing that many who heard him would become casualties of war amplified the urgency of his sermons. His wife Gertrude, a talented stenographer, faithfully recorded his messages. After Chambers unexpectedly died of appendicitis in Egypt at age forty-three, Gertrude compiled excerpts from his teaching into the now famous devotional, *My Utmost for His Highest.*

During the late nineteenth and early twentieth centuries, the prevailing thought was that humankind through science, invention, and civilization had reached such heights that war was a bygone relic. This outlook influenced Western churches to popularize the teaching of postmillennialism, an end-times teaching that society would gradually improve through the church's efforts until Christ returned as king. World War I crushed this optimism.

As society reeled, Chamber's walk with God formed the foundation for his stability and influence in a crumbling world.[7] He "soaked before God"—absorbing the truths of God's Word. Then, the difficulties of his time wrung out the excess into blessings for both his hearers in the desert as well as his readers today.

Have you learned to soak before God? Are you spending enough time with God so that you absorb His perspective on what is going on around you? God promises, "Draw near to God, and He will draw near to you" (James 4:8). Do you so desire to be with God that you, like David, say, "My heart and my flesh cry out for the living God" (Psalm 84:2)? Are you so close to God that you are saturated with His likeness?

How can you be ready to follow God's leading through trials instead of spinning your wheels in frustration? Before difficulties come, root yourself in God's Word. Ground your life in a pattern of dependence on Him. Take time to soak before God.

PERSONAL REFLECTION

- What spiritual habits am I developing now that will strengthen me and allow me to encourage others during difficult times?
- As the thinking of society changes, how can I keep God's Word as the anchor for my soul so that I do not drift away from God on tides of popular opinion?
- Where do I go when I want to soak before God and spend time alone with Him and His Word?

FURTHER READING   Psalm 84

McCasland, David. *Oswald Chambers: Abandoned to God: The Life Story of the Author of My Utmost for His Highest.* Grand Rapids, MI: Discovery House, 1993.

THE HEART OF TEAMWORK

"Prayer—secret fervent believing prayer—lies at the root of all personal godliness. A competent knowledge of the language where a missionary lives, a mild and winning temper, a heart given up to God in closet religion—these, these are the attainments which, more than all knowledge, or all other gifts, will fit us to become the instruments of God in the great work of human redemption." [1]

—WILLIAM WARD, MISSIONARY TO INDIA (1769–1823)

"Endeavoring to keep the unity of the Spirit in the bond of peace."

—EPHESIANS 4:3

B anish them from India immediately!" The order came as soon as William Carey's reinforcements arrived on October 13, 1799. The British East India Company controlled the port and barred missionaries from entering India.

Twenty-nine-year-old William Ward and twelve more missionary recruits had attempted to enter India the same way Carey had seven years earlier.[2] They disembarked before the *Criterion* docked in Kolkata, engaging two smaller boats to smuggle them inland.[3] When word of their arrival leaked out, reporters for the *Calcutta Gazette* mixed up the term *Baptist* with *papist*, referring to followers of the pope. Now, suspicions ran wild that the new missionaries were actually spies for Roman Catholic France and her emperor, Napoleon.[4]

When British officials tracked the alleged spies fifteen miles upstream to Danish-controlled Serampore, the newcomers boldly declared their intentions. They planned to join Carey further inland in Mudnabati where he had prepared an indigo plantation to serve as their base of operations. The British East India Company would have none of it. Though Carey had slipped through their dragnet, his new teammates would not. As soon as they set foot outside the boundaries of Serampore, the British would expel them.

As the travelers, weary from four months at sea, awaited their fate, God intervened. The Danish governor of Serampore, Colonel Ole Bie, defied his British neighbors and offered the missionaries asylum. The governor invited them to establish their headquarters under his jurisdiction, open schools, plant churches, and set up their printing house for the translated Bibles. In addition, he would grant them passports which would allow them freedom to travel across India under Danish protection.[5] This open door not only gave the new missionaries a place of refuge, but also provided Carey and his team a stable base for mission outreach for the rest of their lives.

William Ward, an experienced printer, had first heard of the mission to India from Carey himself seven years before. In March

1793, the two men had walked along the Thames River in London, discussing Carey's imminent departure and his dreams of translating the Bible into the languages of India. "You must come and print it for us," said Carey.[6] But Carey's words faded with time as Ward pursued a profitable career and lent his voice and print shop to William Wilberforce's campaign to abolish the slave trade.[7]

However, when word reached England that Carey had completed his Bengali translation of the New Testament, Ward answered the call to join Carey as the growing team's printer. In October 1798, Ward wrote to Carey:

> I know not whether you will remember a young man, a printer, walking with you from Rippon's Chapel one Sunday, and conversing with you on your journey to India. But that Person is coming to see you, and writes this letter. . . . Sometime in spring I hope to embark with the others. It is in my heart to live and die with you, to spend and be spent with you [2 Corinthians 12:15]. . . . May God make me faithful unto death, giving me patience, fortitude and zeal for the great undertaking.[8]

Three months later, Ward sailed for India.[9]

Soon after Carey and his team settled in Serampore, Ward began printing the Bengali New Testament. In a letter to friends in England, Ward could not contain his enthusiasm: "To give to a man a New Testament who never saw it, who has been reading lies as the Word of God; to give him those everlasting lines which angels would be glad to read—this, this is my blessed work." [10] What satisfaction can be found in using God-given talents for God in His work!

Though printing was Ward's primary role, his responsibilities on the missionary team included much more than his trade. He evangelized, preached the Word, and helped to raise the many children at the headquarters.[11] In addition, as Carey organized their operation, he asked Ward to draft what would become the *Serampore Form of Agreement*.[12] This document outlined the team's working and living relationship.

In this agreement, Ward and the team emphasized the necessity of each member's individual walk with God. In Article 10 of the document, he wrote,

> Let us often look at [David] Brainerd in the woods of America pouring out his very soul before God for the perishing heathen without whose salvation nothing could make him happy. Prayer—secret fervent believing prayer—lies at the root of all personal godliness. A competent knowledge of the language where a missionary lives, a mild and winning temper, a heart given up to God in closet religion [personal devotions]—these, these are the attainments which, more than all knowledge, or all other gifts, will fit us to become the instruments of God in the great work of human redemption.[13]

This emphasis on the inner life and walk with God would form the foundation for their unity as a missionary team and for their work that had only just begun to sprout the first buds of fruit.

What is the key to working with others in the Lord's work? God must be at the center. A common goal may keep a team together for a time. However, a humble walk with God will bind souls together, despite generational gaps, methodological differences, or conflicting preferences.[14] As each person on a team becomes more Christlike, their unity will increase. The apostle Paul puts it this way: "Till we all come to the unity of the faith and of the knowledge of the Son of God, to a perfect man, to the measure of the stature of the fullness of Christ" (Ephesians 4:13). Christ is our head. The closer we walk with Him and fulfill the role He gave us, the more unity and effectiveness we will have as we serve together.

Carey and Ward would find this to be true. Their team in Serampore would multiply what Carey had begun. Thousands of Indians would believe on Christ after reading the Bibles that Carey translated and Ward printed. Alone, neither Carey nor Ward could have made such a difference for God in India. Together, as each maintained his "secret fervent believing prayer," they experienced God's abundant reward for their efforts.

PERSONAL REFLECTION

- How can I put God at the center of all my relationships, especially with my family and my coworkers?
- How can I plan for more time alone with God? How can His influence on my life become more obvious?
- What practical skills do I have that God could use in His work where I live now or on a foreign mission field? How can I sharpen these abilities while gaining ministry training and experience?

FURTHER READING   Ephesians 4:1–16

GODLY ATTRACTION

"I still continued to make the subject a matter of prayer."
—MARIA DYER TAYLOR, MISSIONARY TO CHINA (1837–1870)

"Pursue righteousness, faith, love, peace with those
who call on the Lord out of a pure heart."
—2 TIMOTHY 2:22

Maria Taylor jumped off the balcony. Flames roared from her new home in Yangzhou, China, making a fall from the second story the lesser of two evils. She hit the ground, the impact only partially absorbed by Henry Reid, her coworker who had promised to catch her. Pain shot up Maria's side as blood began to soak her clothing.

A couple more thuds announced the arrival of two more coworkers from the balcony above. Even on the ground, danger surrounded them. The angry mob of local Chinese ruffians that had set their building ablaze now approached Maria and her coworkers from every side. A flying brick staggered Reid, blood pouring from his eye. Stones rained down around them.

The missionaries fled. The less injured coworkers supported Maria and Reid as they ran into the night, dodging missiles as they went. A kind Chinese neighbor, seeing their plight, whisked them into an inner room in his home where the hunted missionaries waited for the crowd to disperse. Soon, other coworkers and their children joined them in hiding.

Though feeling faint from her injuries, Maria Taylor, age thirty-one and gaunt from chronic tuberculosis, sought to comfort the children.[1] Yet, she, too, needed comfort. Where was her husband, Hudson Taylor? Had the Mandarin, the mayor of the town, detained her husband when he went to the government buildings for help earlier that afternoon? Maria later wrote, "I was anxious not to let anyone know how much I was hurt, as I felt it would alarm them, and it seemed most important that all should keep calm. . . . But God was our stay. This confidence He gave me, that He would surely work good for China out of our deep distress."[2] Maria turned to God in prayer for strength. Hours later, God answered her prayers. Her husband returned with government officials to disperse the rioters and secure what was left of their mission house.

Maria well knew the danger when she and her husband forged into inland China with the gospel. The local residents of Yangzhou, isolated from the outside world for centuries, eyed the foreign missionaries with distrust. Rumors swirled about missionaries being devils and even eating children. The tensions culminated with this riot on August 22–23, 1868.

Maria was no stranger to uncertainty and danger. She had spent her early years in China where her parents served as missionaries. Before she turned ten years old, both her father and mother had passed away, and she had moved to Britain for schooling. At age eighteen, Maria chose to return to China to teach in a mission school in Ningbo, not far from Shanghai.

Soon Maria met Hudson and grew to respect his character and dedication. Unknown to her, Hudson also secretly admired her. In their journals, both Maria and Hudson used the same phrase, writing that they would make their relationship "a matter of prayer." Maria wrote, "Before he [Hudson] left I had some little reason, perhaps, to think that he might be interested in me but I thought I had better not be too sanguine. I still continued to make the subject a matter of prayer." At the same time, Hudson wrote, "I did not move in the matter [whether or not to pursue Maria], and in the latter part of January went up to Shanghai, making it a matter of prayer as before."[3] Yet, as their relationship grew and she prepared for marriage, Maria wrote: "If he [Hudson] loves me more than Jesus he is not worthy of me—if he were to leave the Lord's work for the world's honour, I would have nothing further to do with him."[4] That love for Christ and dedication to His work would draw Hudson and Maria together and make them a dynamic team.

Just over ten years before the fiery attack in Yangchow, Hudson proposed to Maria near Shanghai. He warned her of the risk of marrying him: "I cannot hold you to your promise [to marry me] if you would rather draw back. You see how difficult our life may be at times." Maria had no qualms: "Have you forgotten? I was left an orphan in a far-off land. God has been my Father all these years. Do you think I shall be afraid to trust Him now?"[5] Life with Hudson would be a continuation of the life she had already chosen. Her reliance on God and prayer life would sustain her as before. Hudson and Maria's relationship, built on their individual prayer lives, would combine in joint intercession for their new family and the beginning of the faith missions movement.[6]

Maria became the "Mother of the China Inland Mission."[7] She supported her husband when many abandoned him. Her calm influence helped to further mature Hudson as a man and as a missionary. She encouraged him to follow the Lord's leading in establishing a truly unique mission made of working-class believers from many denominations. She helped her husband write pamphlets like "China: Its Spiritual Need and Claims" in 1865, which greatly influenced men and women to join them to reach inland China. Alongside her husband on furlough in England, she recruited and trained the founding missionaries of the CIM.

Nearly two years after the Yangzhou riot, Maria's work on earth came to a close. Her husband watched as tuberculosis and an intestinal disease stole her strength away. In the days after her death, Hudson wrote of his love for Maria and specifically noted their times of prayer together:

> He [God] and He only knew what my dear wife was to me. He knew how the light of my eyes and the joy of my heart were in her. On the last day of her life (we had no idea that it would prove the last) our hearts were mutually delighted by the never old story of each other's love. . . . But [God] saw that it was good to take her; good indeed for her, and in His love He took her painlessly; and not less good for me who must henceforth toil and suffer alone—yet not alone, for God is nearer to me than ever. And now I have to tell Him all my sorrows and difficulties, as I used to tell dear Maria; and as she cannot join me in intercession, to rest in the knowledge of Jesus' intercession; to

walk a little less by feeling, a little less by sight, a little more by faith [2 Corinthians 5:7].[8]

Without Maria—her influence on Hudson's interactions with others, her care for her husband's health, her selfless commitment to the work, and especially her prayers with her husband—the China Inland Mission may never have existed.

Who you choose to be your spouse or your closest friends reveals much about you. God urges His people to "pursue righteousness, faith, love, peace with those who call on the Lord out of a pure heart" (2 Timothy 2:22). Do you surround yourself with those who will urge you closer to the Savior? Will those who spend time with you find themselves drawn closer to God? Does your influence lead to others serving the Lord more effectively?

PERSONAL REFLECTION

- What attracts me to other people? What traits in my closest friends do I consider more important than godliness and passion for Christ? What does this say about me?
- How can I become the kind of person that will be attractive to those with pure hearts?
- How vital is prayer to my personal relationships?

FURTHER READING 2 Timothy 2:19–26

Pollock, John. *Hudson Taylor and Maria: A Match Made in Heaven.* Fearn, Ross-shire, Scotland: Christian Focus Publications, 1996.

NOT LOST TIME TO WAIT ON GOD

"It is not lost time to wait on God."[1]

—J. HUDSON TAYLOR, MISSIONARY TO CHINA (1832–1905)

"Stand still and see the salvation of the Lord, who is with you,
O Judah and Jerusalem! Do not fear or be dismayed . . .
for the Lord is with you."

—2 CHRONICLES 20:17

Paralyzed. Forty-two-year-old Hudson Taylor could not move from the waist down. The doctors of London restricted him to bed rest but gave him little hope of recovery.

Months before, on a steamboat on the Yangtze River in China, Taylor had slipped off a ladder down into the hold of the ship. The impact on his heels jolted his spine. Pain knifed through his back. The next few days, Taylor hobbled with a cane.

The growth of the China Inland Mission and the recent passing of a key member of the home office staff demanded that Taylor return to London in August of 1874. In transit, his pain increased.

Once in London, his mobility decreased to the point where he could not even turn himself over in bed.

All around Taylor, God's work went on without him. The preaching of D. L. Moody had revived Christians and churches across the United Kingdom. A renewed emphasis on spiritual life coincided with this awakening. Such an atmosphere was prime for recruiting more missionaries for China's unreached millions. Yet, the leader of the China Inland Mission could do little from his bed—little but pray.

For an hour or two each day, Taylor did what he could, when his physical condition allowed it. Flat on his back, he dictated letters for the mission and pamphlets for recruitment. He encouraged everyone to pray that God would send eighteen new missionaries to China like He had sent twenty-four nearly ten years before. Yet, Taylor had no strength for the urgent needs at hand—the reorganization of the home office and recruitment of new missionaries for the far-flung, unreached provinces. Months passed as he stared up at the map of China that hung from the posts at the end of his bed.

Taylor may have been confined, but God was not. During Taylor's convalescence, God sent volunteers, old friends and new, to sustain the home office. Taylor reported,

> The Mission had no paid helpers but God led volunteers, without pre-arrangement, to come in from day to day to write from dictation, and thus letters were answered. If one who called in the morning could not stay long enough to answer all, another was sure to come, and perhaps one or two might look in in the afternoon. Occasionally, a young friend who was employed in the city would come after business hours and do

any needful bookkeeping, or finish letters not already dealt with. So it was day by day. One of the happiest periods of my life was that period of forced inactivity, when one could do nothing but "rejoice in the Lord" [Philippians 4:4] and "wait patiently for Him," [Psalm 37:7] and see Him meeting all one's need. Never were my letters, before or since, kept so regularly and promptly answered.

God not only got the work done, but He did it better than Taylor could have.

As God gathered the eighteen recruits, He gradually increased Taylor's strength to prepare them for departure for China.

> And the eighteen men asked of God began to come. There was first some correspondence; then they came to see me in my room. Soon I had a class studying Chinese at my bedside. In due time the Lord sent them forth, and then the dear friends at Mildmay [just south of Nottingham in central England] began to pray for my restoration. The Lord blessed the means used and I was raised up. One reason for my being laid aside was gone. Had I been well and able to move about, some might have thought that my urgent appeals rather than God's working had sent the eighteen men to China. But utterly laid aside, able only to dictate a request for prayer, the answer to our prayers was the more apparent. [2]

Taylor rejoiced that God received all the glory. The paralyzed man in the bed was God's instrument. Truly, God's strength is made perfect in weakness.

Ten months after his arrival in London, Taylor testified,

> When I came home, I hoped to have done much for China. God soon put that out of the question, as you know, and for

many long months there was little I could do but pray. And what has been the result? Far more has been done by God; far more is being done, far more will be done by Him than my most sanguine hopes ventured to anticipate. And shall we learn no lesson from this? Shall we not each one of us determine to labour more in prayer; to cultivate more intimate communion with God by His help; thinking less of our working and more of His working, that He may in very deed be glorified in and through us? If we can and will do this, I am quite sure that ere long there will be abundant evidence of it in the improved state of our congregations and churches, in the preparedness of the people for the message, and in the power with which it is delivered. More souls will be saved; the believers will lead more holy lives, and our own knowledge of God and joy in Him will be multiplied. Surely we ought to lead beautiful lives, glorious lives, if we are really with Him Who is Chiefest among Ten Thousand, the Altogether Lovely! "The people that do know their God shall be strong and do exploits" (Daniel 11:32).[3]

Taylor's relationship with God sustained him, shaped his outlook on his trial, and strengthened him for future exploits.

After nearly five months on his back and another five months of gradual recovery, God completely healed Taylor. When circumstances look most impossible, God is at work. Taylor often said, "There are commonly three stages in work for God: first impossible, then difficult, then done."[4] Despite Taylor's incapacity, God still accomplished His work. In September of 1876, Taylor boarded a ship and returned with eight more new missionaries to lead the expanding mission in China.

When God allows circumstances in your life that keep you from doing what you think He wants you to do, wait on Him.

Raging against your powerlessness will solve nothing. As the prophet Jahaziel encouraged King Jehoshaphat, "Do not be afraid nor dismayed because of this great multitude, for the battle is not yours, but God's" (2 Chronicles 20:15). Be assured that God will accomplish His work. Calm your spirit with the truths of God's Word: "Wait on the Lord; Be of good courage, And He shall strengthen your heart; Wait, I say, on the Lord" (Psalm 27:14). Taylor would later attest, "It is not lost time to wait on God." When you rely on Him, He does so much more than you could ever do, and He gets all the glory.

PERSONAL REFLECTION

- What is happening in my life today that is teaching me to wait on the Lord?
- How can I better redeem time that appears to be wasted by factors beyond my control?
- If God works through me, but few people know of my labors, do I feel satisfied or undervalued? Why?

FURTHER READING   2 Chronicles 20:1–22

Taylor, Dr. and Mrs. Howard. *Hudson Taylor in Early Years: The Growth of a Soul.* Singapore: OMF International, 1911.

Taylor, Dr. and Mrs. Howard. *Hudson Taylor and the China Inland Mission: The Growth of a Work of God.* Singapore: OMF International, 1918.

WHAT CAME OUT
OF THE HAYSTACK

"Oh, that He would make his children feel their dependence,
and bring them to cast themselves at his footstool! All our
strength is from the Lord."

—SAMUEL J. MILLS, ITINERANT HOME MISSIONARY
AND RECRUITER (1783–1818)

"Seek the Lord and His strength;
Seek His face evermore!"

—1 CHRONICLES 16:11

A bolt of lightning cut through the thunderheads above a grove of maple trees in Sloan's Meadow, Massachusetts. Far from the safety of the buildings on the campus of Williams College, Samuel Mills and his classmates looked for shelter from the storm. On a sweltering August afternoon in 1806, they had gathered in this quiet place to pray and brainstorm about the possibility of foreign missions.

With excitement, Mills and his friends discussed the spiritual needs of the Indians, Turks, and Arabs. American Christians well knew the missionary work of John Eliot and David Brainerd. They admired the overseas endeavors of the British, especially the recent exploits of William Carey in India and the London Missionary Society's bold advance in the South Pacific. To their knowledge, no Americans had left their own shores as missionaries.[1]

A loud peal of thunder interrupted their conversation again. The dull roar of an approaching downpour sent the young men scrambling for cover. Beyond the maple grove, the trees gave way to the fields of a New England farm.

"Come, let us make it a subject of prayer under the haystack," said Mills.[2] The young men burrowed into the haystack, carving a small prayer room. There, Mills continued to encourage his companions. The light can dispel the darkness, he argued. Let's not fear the danger or be daunted by the obstacles. "We can do it if we will," he told them.

Mills' words were neither conceited nor naive. Writing in his journal a few months earlier on June 26, 1806, Mills explained his confidence: "The work is the Lord's, and he is abundantly able to carry it on. Arise, O Lord, thou and the ark of thy strength! [Psalm 132:8]"[3] In another entry, Mills wrote, "Oh, that He would make his children feel their dependence, and bring them to cast themselves at his footstool! All our strength is from the Lord."[4] In the stuffiness of their haystack refuge, the young men prayed that God would remove the obstacles for the spread of the gospel across the world. They begged God to send them as missionaries.

"The Haystack Prayer Meeting," as it came to be known in church history, marked the beginning of the first missions movement in the United States.[5] The missions prayer meetings at Williams College continued.[6] As Mills moved on to Yale briefly and then Andover Seminary, more young men joined his meetings, including the recently converted Adoniram Judson.

By 1810, Mills and his companions felt ready to go overseas. Since no American mission board existed, Mills aggressively drummed up support for the cause. On June 27, 1810, a group of pastors, university professors, and students met in Bradford, Massachusetts, where they established the Board of Commissioners for Foreign Missions, the first American mission board.[7]

However, the fledgling mission society had few supporters and not nearly enough funds. Impatient to launch a mission to Asia, Judson inquired into the possibility of serving under the London Missionary Society. The idea appalled Mills:

> What! Is England to support her own missionaries and ours likewise? . . . Perhaps the fathers [older pastors in New England] will soon arise and take the business of missions into their own hands. But should they hesitate, let us be prepared to GO FORWARD,—trusting to that God for assistance who hath said, "Lo, I am with you always, even to the end of the world [Matthew 28:20]."[8]

God had raised up the missionary candidates and the American board. He would soon supply the funds for the first missionaries from the United States.

When the new missionaries embarked for Kolkata, India, on February 19, 1812, Mills was not on the ship. With funds still limited, Mills felt that other men were more qualified than he, especially since they had graduated from seminary before him.

Furthermore, the new board decided Mills' talents for recruiting others into missions were needed in America. This became his life's work.[9]

Wherever he went, Mills explored the spiritual need of an area, published that need enthusiastically, and a wave of missionaries followed. The first band, which included Adoniram and Ann Judson, traveled to Asia. Another wave of Christian ministers followed Mills' two investigative missionary journeys to the Mississippi Valley (modern-day Louisiana to Missouri).[10]

When the mission passed over Mills for a post in Sri Lanka in 1815, Mills plunged into inner-city work along the east coast of the United States.[11] Once again, men and women answered his call.[12] In addition, Mills became instrumental in furthering gospel work among native American peoples and exploring possible avenues toward freedom for African-American slaves.[13]

In 1818, thirty-five-year-old Mills lost a battle with malaria which he contracted on a survey trip to the west coast of Africa. Yet even in death, his recruitment continued. A short biography of his life compelled others to leave their homeland for missionary work overseas.[14]

Why did people follow Samuel Mills into the Lord's work? He lacked both a charismatic personality and a dynamic speaking ability.[15] However, Mills' genuine piety and infectious enthusiasm inspired those around him. He championed the immortality of the soul of every person regardless of social class, ethnicity, or geographic location. He believed in the power of God's Word and walked in dependence on God. In a journal entry on June 28, 1806, Mills wrote, "Oh, for more fervor, more engagedness, more activity in the cause of the blessed God!"[16] Like David at the Tabernacle in Jerusalem, Mills urged those around him to follow the Lord:

Give thanks unto the LORD, call upon his name, make known his deeds among the people. Sing unto him, sing psalms unto him, talk ye of all his wondrous works. Glory ye in his holy name: let the heart of them rejoice that seek the LORD. Seek the LORD and his strength, seek his face continually [1 Chronicles 16:8–11].

A fervent passion ignited by his walk with God drove Mills to influence others.

Not all of those who are zealous for missions end up overseas. History recounts the valiant efforts of men like Mills who urged others to go and supported them as they went. William Carey had Samuel Pearce, John Ryland, and John Sutcliffe behind him in England. Hudson Taylor had Benjamin Broomhall, laboring behind the scenes in London, and George Müller, supporting the mission financially. Today, pastors and Christians encourage and support missionaries in the darkest corners of the world.

Whether or not God leads you to serve Him overseas, a passion for missions should breed action wherever God has placed you. No matter where you are, God has called you to share His gospel, disciple His people, and glorify His name. Your burning love for God and others should leave a trail of influence for God behind you. Who knows what future doors will open because of your faithfulness where you are now?

PERSONAL REFLECTION

- Are Christ and His work a dominant focus in my life and conversation? What are my favorite topics to discuss with others?
- What should I eliminate from my life so that my passion for God and His work can burn more brightly?
- Do the friends with whom I surround myself push me closer to Christ and inspire me to serve Him?

FURTHER READING Acts 11:19–26

Richards, Thomas C. *Samuel J. Mills: Missionary Pathfinder, Pioneer, and Promoter*. Boston: The Pilgrim Press, 1906.

THE HISTORY OF ANSWERED PRAYER

"The history of missions is the history of answered prayer."
—SAMUEL ZWEMER, MISSIONARY TO IRAQ, BAHRAIN, AND EGYPT (1867–1952)

"Now this is the confidence that we have in Him, that if we ask anything according to His will, He hears us. And if we know that He hears us, whatever we ask, we know that we have the petitions that we have asked of Him."
—1 JOHN 5:14–15

Sharks circled the ship as the rough waves of the Persian Gulf battered its hull and splashed over the railing. Despite the tempestuous seas, a sailor hauled a drum on deck and began beating it with a stick. Twenty-three-year-old Samuel Zwemer and his Syrian companion, Kamil Abdul Messiah, could not imagine how a drum solo could improve their situation.

"It's a shark drum," the sailor-turned-performer shouted in Arabic over the crash of the waves. "The sharks are now afraid." [1]

Sharks were not the only danger for Zwemer as he searched for a location to serve as base of operations for his gospel outreach in the Middle East. On this trip, his first missionary journey in early 1891, Zwemer had already visited Jeddah and various ports along the Arabian coast of the Red Sea. However, he and Kamil Messiah decided to go further. They pushed on to Yemen, Oman, and beyond—lands virtually unreached with the gospel. [2]

As Zwemer and Messiah prayed aboard the ship, three Muslim men overheard them. Zwemer relates that they "came to ask for copies of these prayers to use themselves, as they said they liked them better than those they used. The next day, they were reading and learning the Christian prayers that Kamil had copied for them." [3] God gave Kamil great boldness in selling Arabic Scripture pamphlets which the ship captain, crew, and passengers eagerly bought and read.

Upon arrival in Mukalla, Yemen, Zwemer and Messiah continued distributing Christian literature until their supply ran out. Zwemer reports of his coworker's zeal: "Kamil [Messiah] was busy all the time in the house and in the market, proving from the Scriptures (theirs and ours) that Jesus Christ is the Prophet Who has come into the world and that salvation is in Him alone." [4] On his return to their temporary base in Aden, Yemen, Zwemer reported, "The best and the sweetest and the most delicious of all the glad tidings which we have written is this: We have planted in the Lord's vineyard, in this blessed journey, one hundred and ten copies of the Arabic Scriptures." [5] They spread the seed, trusting God's promise not to let His Word return void (Isaiah 55:11).

Whether facing vicious weather, religious persecution, or even deadly disease, Samuel Zwemer believed in the power of prayer. He famously said,

> Since the beginning of the missionary enterprise in the upper room at Jerusalem, prayer has been the secret of power and perseverance and victory. The history of missions is the history of answered prayer. From Pentecost to the Haystack meeting in New England and from the days when Robert Morrison landed in China to the martyrdom of John and Betty Stam, prayer has been the source of power and the secret of spiritual triumph.[6]

In Zwemer's mind, prayer was essential to accomplish Great Commission work.

As a young man, Zwemer cultivated a daily pattern of time alone with God. At age twenty-one, he wrote, "George Müller's life of trust makes one feel the power of prayer. Why can we not all live in that way?"[7] The teaching of Scripture and the example of those who went before him shaped Zwemer's walk with God and led to the daring and passion that would characterize his life and ministry.

In late 1912, twenty-one years after he began his pioneer work based in Iraq and then Bahrain, Zwemer followed God's leading to Cairo, Egypt. He spent the next seventeen years directing the Nile Mission Press, training leaders in a Bible institute, and overseeing the ongoing work of the Arabian Mission he had begun. Zwemer also wrote extensively and traveled the world, recruiting missionaries to Muslim lands.

These various responsibilities allowed Zwemer to touch the lives of many. Soon after Zwemer arrived in Cairo, young William Borden, who had caught the vision for Muslim work while

hearing Zwemer preach in the U.S., joined his recruiter for training. When the young man unexpectedly passed away in 1913,
Zwemer prayed at his funeral.[8] Later that same year, Lilias Trotter
spent a month in Cairo. Zwemer's Nile Mission Press eventually
published many of her Arabic tracts and books.[9] He also visited
Trotter's work in Algeria in 1922.

World War I brought thousands of soldiers to Egypt, and
Zwemer assisted the YMCA in preaching the gospel to them
and recruiting them into future Muslim work. During this time,
Zwemer crossed paths with Oswald Chambers. Zwemer's daugh-
ter played the piano for Chambers' evangelistic meetings, and
Zwemer also attended Chambers' funeral.[10]

Though visible fruit was meager and missionary casualties,
even among his own family, were high, Zwemer counted on God
to act as He had in the past in response to the prayers of His people. Zwemer writes,

> William Carey, Henry Martyn, David Livingstone, David
> Brainerd, Mary Moffat, Mary Slessor, James Gilmour—what
> diversities of gifts and tasks and environment! Yet in one gift
> of the Spirit they all had a large share, the gift of prayer and
> intercession. As one reads these biographies, again and again the
> narrative is eloquent with testimony to God's miraculous power
> in answer to prayer.[11]

With faith in God's promise, Zwemer brimmed with confidence:
"Just as sure as are the promises of God is the certainty that He
will gather out a people for His Name from Arabia."[12] Zwemer
passed this vision on to scores of young men and women who
followed him to the Middle East and beyond.

How certain are you that God answers prayer? Do you not trust God's promises to hear His children? 1 John 5:14–15 says, "Now this is the confidence that we have in Him, that if we ask anything according to His will, He hears us. And if we know that He hears us, whatever we ask, we know that we have the petitions that we have asked of Him." Do you have this confidence? Do you know what God has revealed in His Word to be His will so that you can pray in concert with Him? Is not the salvation of souls God's expressed will (2 Peter 3:9)? Is not the development of personal holiness clearly God's desire for His children (1 Thessalonians 4:3)? Is not spiritual fruit God's will (John 15:16)? May your confidence in God's answer to your prayers match the audacity of His promises.

PERSONAL REFLECTION

- How can I pray more specifically so that my life can become a history of answered prayer?
- When God answers my prayers, how often do I remember what He has done and tell others the story of how God worked?
- How can my prayers better express my dependence on God to work in difficult environments?

FURTHER READING   Acts 12

Wilson, J. Christy. *Apostle to Islam: A Biography of Samuel M. Zwemer*. Grand Rapids: Baker Book House, 1952.

HARDSHIP, THE SCHOOL OF PRAYER

"By complaining I cannot bring myself a step nearer to God."
—HANNAH MARSHMAN, THE FIRST WOMAN MISSIONARY
TO INDIA (1767–1847)

"When my soul fainted within me,
I remembered the Lord;
And my prayer went up to You,
Into Your holy temple."
—JONAH 2:7

Chaos swirled around Hannah Marshman during her first few weeks in India. While the Serampore Trio—William Carey, William Ward, and her husband, Joshua Marshman—arranged to acquire their new headquarters, somebody had to provide for the day-to-day needs of the new team. As ten adults and nine children moved into a dilapidated compound, who would oversee the meals and domestic affairs?[1]

The growing community of missionaries faced grave obstacles. As Hannah had been warned, mental illness had incapacitated Dorothy Carey, and the teenage Carey boys clearly lacked supervision. Then, just three weeks after Hannah arrived, coworker William Grant passed away, leaving a widow and two children. Within a few months, a second coworker, John Fountain, also died. His new bride who had sailed with Hannah aboard the *Criterion* to India became a single mother before her child was born. Hannah herself had three children that she needed to comfort as they adjusted to the sweltering heat and vastly different culture of India.

With so many needs, Hannah took charge of the domestic side of the mission.[2] The veteran missionary Carey led the team and translated the Scriptures. Ward provided the printing expertise. Her husband launched their educational endeavors. Behind the scenes, Hannah kept everyone fed and the environment livable. She comforted the widows among them. She and Ward helped to raise the Carey boys.[3] Hannah even bathed Dorothy Carey. As the first evidences of spiritual fruit began to blossom among the Indian people in the early 1800s, the unsung hero behind the work was the mother of the mission, Hannah Marshman.[4]

However, Hannah's role included much more than domestic oversight. She was also an educator. Just months after her arrival, Hannah and her husband, Joshua, opened a school for Eurasian boys and girls.[5] Hannah wrote to a friend about the decision to add this undertaking to her already long list of responsibilities:

> I searched my mind very minutely before I engaged in the School, lest it should be irksome to me afterwards. However I was enabled to leave all, and thankfully to give myself up to

the work; and through mercy I have not repented [changed my mind], and hope I never may. I am not worthy of being employed in anything belonging to Christ. . . . I long for the increase of Christ's kingdom upon earth.[6]

This school was the first of many educational endeavors the couple pursued together, including free schools for the poor.[7]

As Hannah's work increased, so did her family. Hannah gave birth to twelve children. However, consistent with the high infant mortality rate of the time, only six reached adulthood. When her infant daughter Rachel fell ill in August 1804, Hannah wrote in her journal, "May she be restored if consistent with the will of Him who gave her to me; but if otherwise may I cheerfully submit to his will: I welcome all that brings me near to him."[8] Rachel survived to write the memoir that records her mother's words.

While she found fulfillment in her various roles, Hannah's self-assessments were not always positive. On October 13, 1804, she recorded a rather severe personal review:

> Five years ago I first set my foot on the shores of India. The time seems short to look back, but oh, what have I done in all this time that has been acceptable to God? Nothing, nothing in comparison to what I ought to have done. In the course of these five years which are past, many changing scenes have taken place, much affliction both in the family and the Church: but more abundant mercy. Conviction work has been begun, and some precious souls have been brought to the knowledge of the Saviour.[9]

Even when struggling spiritually, Hannah reminded herself, "By complaining I cannot bring myself a step nearer to God. He is gracious in all his ways, and holy in all his works, and his Word says 'Seek and ye shall find' [Matthew 6:33]. I will wait upon him."[10] She daily praised God: "Experienced another day's mercies from the hands of God, he is the giver of all good to me . . . his word and promises are my hope, in myself I have nothing, I am nothing."[11] As she encouraged herself with God's Word, Hannah persevered.

In 1807, Hannah established the first school for Indian women in the history of the country. She believed that with increased literacy more women and families would come to Christ. By 1819, she had formed the Serampore Native Female Education Society. In just five years, this organization reproduced her women's school in thirteen new locations across India, including Chittagong, Dacca, Allahabad, and Delhi.[12] Other missions followed her lead, expanding the movement for female education.

During forty-seven years of labor in India, Hannah's prayer life and dependence on God deepened.[13] In one particularly difficult period, she wrote, "I am ready to wish I had never come to this country, but surely it was not my own seeking; I came because I thought it was the will of God, and think so still, and will therefore endeavor to do my duty with cheerfulness, looking to him for strength and direction in all things, and praying to be kept from sinning in the present case [this time of discouragement]."[14] Commenting on her later years, her pastor in India noted Hannah's devotion to prayer:

> One feature in [Hannah's] character must not be omitted: . . . the spirit of prayer. . . . she fervently prayed for her children, for the church and congregation meeting here, for her neighbours, European and native—for the young people, minister, schools—emphatically and distinctly.[15]

In the crucible of hardship, Hannah had learned the necessity of prayer and reliance on God.

During an age when Carey outlived three wives and Adoniram Judson in nearby Burma was survived by only his third wife, Hannah Marshman outlived all her coworkers.[16] She dedicated her life to serving God, her husband, her children, her teammates, her teammates' children, and the Indian people—especially their women.

History rings with the praises of William Carey, Joshua Marshman, and William Ward—the faithful team that pioneered the gospel in India. Few speak of the woman who filled in the gaps between them. Her role in the education and evangelization of Indian women remains unsung. Yet, the Serampore Trio could well have been called the Serampore Quartet.[17]

Today, many women like Hannah Marshman serve without recognition. They are "keepers at home" (Titus 2:5). They teach children in the back room while others stand on stage. They cook while others eat. They care for those whom others neglect and devalue—young mothers, widows, children, orphans, and the elderly. These dedicated ladies endure hardship and trials with little complaining. They learn to pray because only God is listening. Though they often do not feel it, such faithful women's influence reaches far beyond the recognition they receive in this life. God says the price of these virtuous and godly women is "far beyond rubies" (Proverbs 31:10).

Find your value in God's assessment. Seek your satisfaction in serving others. Spend your time in what God has placed before you. When the road gets tough, persevere by the power of prayer. Make yourself quietly indispensable, behind the scenes changing the world.

PERSONAL REFLECTION

- What women in my life have had the greatest spiritual influence on me? Why?
- When others do not value my role and efforts, how should I respond as a servant of God?
- When I work hard and no one notices, what will keep me praying instead of complaining?

FURTHER READING   1 Samuel 1:1–2:11

TRY AND TRUST

*"There are two little words in our language
which I have always admired, TRY and TRUST."*[1]

—JOHN WILLIAMS, MISSIONARY TO OCEANIA (1796–1839)

*"'Lord, if it is You, command me to come to You
on the water.' So He said, 'Come.'"*

—MATTHEW 14:28–29A

I need a boat," said twenty-two-year-old John Williams. In 1817, less than a year before, John Williams and his wife Mary had arrived in the South Pacific. They made their new home on the island of Raiatea, just west of Tahiti, but already Williams eyed the neighboring island of Tahaa where people had never heard the gospel.[2]

God had gifted this Welshman with the ability to watch and learn, especially with mechanical things. As a youth in England, he had spent weeks observing the machinists in a shop where he managed the business. Just by watching, he learned to do the intricate work himself. Aboard the ship from England through Rio de Janeiro and Sydney to Tahiti, Williams had observed every aspect of the ship, how it worked, and how to sail it. Now, with the need for a boat, Williams tried to build his own. Soon, he sailed to Tahaa in his handmade, sixteen-foot vessel.

Though he loved to work with his hands, Williams' true passion lay elsewhere. He had one goal:

> My work is my delight. In it I desire to spend and to be spent [2 Corinthians 12:15]. I think and hope that I have no other desire in my soul than to be the means of winning sinners for Christ. My anxiety is that my tongue may be ever engaged in proclaiming this salvation, and that my words and actions may be always pointing to the Cross! [3]

Williams sought to "preach Christ crucified" (1 Corinthians 1:23). Everything else was a means to this end.[4]

In late 1823, Williams wrote to the London Missionary Society. He needed a bigger ship to take the gospel to the scattered islands beyond the reach of his homemade boat: "For my own part I cannot content myself within the narrow limits of a single reef [the small cluster of islands nearby]; and if means are not afforded, a continent would to me be infinitely preferable, for there if you cannot ride you can walk."[5] However, the London Missionary Society (LMS) was not ready to commission another ship. The *Duff* which had brought Henry Nott and the first generation of LMS missionaries to the South Pacific had been captured by pirates in 1799 and lost forever to the mission.

Undaunted, Williams boarded whatever merchant ship would take him where he needed to go, even if it meant inconvenience and lengthy delays. Earlier that year, he had left the island cluster around Raiatea for Aitutaki in the Cook Islands, over five hundred miles away between Tahiti and Samoa. When he left Aitutaki, two

Polynesian believers he had trained for gospel ministry stayed behind. Later in the year aboard a merchant vessel, Williams discovered Rarotonga, an island that would serve as a major launch point for the gospel.

After eighteen months, Williams returned to Aitutaki.[6] He found that God had greatly used the Polynesian believers he had left behind. The islanders had forsaken idolatry, left cannibalism, and built a large church building. Echoing the well-known motto of Carey, Williams wrote, "I hope for great things, pray for great things, and confidently expect great things to result from these labours."[7] If only he had his own ship so he could scatter dedicated Polynesian evangelists across the South Pacific!

Three years later, Williams had not given up his pleas to the LMS for a ship: "Had I a ship at my command, not one island in the Pacific but should, God permitting, be visited, and teachers sent to direct the wandering feet of the heathen to happiness—to heaven."[8] Finally in 1827, with the help of his Polynesian brothers in Christ, Williams built his own ocean-worthy ship—the seventy-ton, sixty-foot vessel, *The Messenger of Peace*.[9]

With a ship at his disposal, Williams' ministry finally transitioned from evangelism and leadership training on one island to making first gospel contact on island after island. Though Williams' imposing height could intimidate the islanders, he attracted them with his friendly demeanor. Williams would often say, "Kindness is the key to the human heart."[10] Islands and hearts opened at his caring efforts. Two by two, Polynesian gospel workers followed in Williams' wake.

Williams encouraged the Polynesian ministers he left on the islands as missionaries: "Work well and pray much. Think of the death of Jesus; and reflect that the natives of the islands to which you go are purchased with His blood." The unsaved residents of these islands "will watch you with rats' eyes, to find little crooked places in your conduct." Therefore, these native missionaries must "remember well your work. Give to it your hands, your mouths, your bodies, your souls, and God bless your labours! In your temporal concerns be diligent. A lazy missionary is both an ugly and a useless being." He exhorted them: "Have singleness of heart to Jesus and His Gospel. Search His Word, and pray to Him." [11] For over a decade, Williams advanced the gospel from island to island across Polynesia.

In 1839, Williams initiated contact in Vanuatu (then called New Hebrides). The locals, having been recently attacked and abused by depraved European traders, took out their revenge on the Welsh missionary who had come to bring God's love. Despite Williams' martyrdom, God's work continued. Nineteen years later, John Paton would arrive in Vanuatu and establish churches across these islands, bearing the fruit that Williams had died to plant. [12]

Throughout his ministry, Williams encouraged his fellow missionaries, whether foreign or Polynesian, to launch out and attempt great things for God:

> There are two little words in our language which I have always admired, TRY and TRUST. You know not what you can or cannot effect until you try; and if you make your trials in the exercise of trust in God, mountains of imaginary difficulty will vanish as you approach them, and facilities will be afforded which you never anticipated. [13]

Williams spoke from personal experience. He launched out and attempted much for God while depending on God to open doors of opportunity for the gospel.

In Matthew 14, Jesus called Peter to step out of the boat in the middle of a storm—to walk on water as Jesus did. Peter tried what eleven other disciples did not dare to attempt, and he did what none of them ever did. Peter walked on water.

Jesus calls every follower today to step out and rely on Him— to try and trust. Do you dare depend on Him like John Williams did? Do not allow obstacles to freeze you to inaction. If you try, you may fail, but you may also succeed. Alternatively, you may discover a path toward God's goals for your life that you would never have otherwise found had you not stepped out. You may find out that the barrier you perceived to be insurmountable was not nearly the roadblock you thought it to be. You may discover that the greatest impediment is your own fearful imagination. However, if you do not try, you are guaranteed to fail, and you will lose the opportunity to learn greater dependence on God.

Like John Williams, let us try and trust.

PERSONAL REFLECTION

- What is stopping me from stepping out to serve God in more significant ways?
- How can I be more resourceful in finding ways to overcome rather than succumbing to what is holding me back in my service to God?
- Why do I not trust God enough to attempt more for Him?

FURTHER READING   Matthew 14:22–33

Ellis, James J. *John Williams: The Martyr Missionary of Polynesia.* New York: Fleming H. Revell, 1889.

LETTING GO

"I shall follow you every day with my prayers."
—MARY WILLIAMS, MISSIONARY TO OCEANIA (1789-1852)

"Trust in the Lord with all your heart,
And lean not on your own understanding;
In all your ways acknowledge Him,
And He shall direct your paths."
—PROVERBS 3:5-6

This was too much. Mary Williams had surrendered to missions, married John, and sailed for the South Pacific in 1817. She lived in a primitive hut among barely dressed islanders on Raiatea in the Cook Islands. Then, she and her growing family followed her husband to Rarotonga, an island he had only recently discovered. She labored beside him to win the Polynesians to Christ. They often traveled as a family to neighboring islands. Wasn't this enough? Now in 1827 after over ten years of hardship, John wanted to sail west without them to the Samoan Islands. Did he have a death wish?

Mary made her point to her husband, and she made it clearly:

> How can you suppose that I can give my consent to such a
> strange proposition? You will be eighteen hundred miles away,
> six months absent, and among the most savage people we are
> acquainted with; and if you should lose your life in the attempt,
> I shall be left a widow with my fatherless children, twenty
> thousand miles from my friends and my home.[1]

John listened to his wife's passionate words. He wrote, "Finding her so decidedly opposed to the undertaking, I did not mention it again, although my mind was still fixed upon the object."[2] God's time had not yet come.

A few months later, Mary fell ill. Without warning, the thirty-eight-year-old woman lay at death's door.[3] Many early missionaries' lives ended like this in the South Pacific. For ten days, John pleaded with the Lord to heal his wife. God answered his prayers.

As Mary lay recovering, she pondered why God had allowed her health to deteriorate so quickly. As she prayed, a thought came to her—maybe she was standing in the way of God's work in Samoa. Maybe God needed to take her from this world so that His will on earth could be accomplished through her husband. Mary called John to her bedside and explained her change of heart: "From this time your desire [to take the gospel to Samoa] has my full concurrence [agreement]; and when you go, I shall follow you every day with my prayers, that God may preserve you from danger, crown your attempt with success, and bring you back in safety."[4] John could not believe his ears. He had not spoken to his wife about Samoa in months. Now, God's time had come.

Immediately, John gave the Samoan mission top priority. In just three months, as his wife regained strength, John and his

Polynesian coworkers built an ocean-worthy ship, *The Messenger of Peace*. After a few shorter voyages, he traversed the nearly two thousand miles to Samoa in 1830 and planted the first seeds of the gospel in these islands. Today, a monument stands in Samoa to commemorate John Williams' pioneer efforts for the gospel.

Throughout this work, John could see God's hand. He often quoted Mark 16:20: "And they went forth and preached everywhere, the Lord working with them." John later reminisced about God's leading in Samoa, remembering first how God had changed his wife's heart:

> Is it possible to reflect upon the manner in which Mrs. Williams gave her consent to this enterprise,—to our meeting with the chief at Tongatabu,—to the death of Tamafaigna,—and to other striking particulars, without exclaiming, "Here is something more than accident. This is the finger of God?". . . It is impossible to reflect upon our first voyage to Samoa, and not discover the hand of God.[5]

Mary Williams' understandable fears for her husband put her at odds with God's plan. When God got her attention through her illness, she realized that, though she had served well and surrendered much for the cause of Christ, she now stood not only in her husband's way but also in God's way. When Mary recognized her error, she immediately repented and submitted to God. She learned the lesson of Proverbs 3:5–6: "Trust in the Lord with all your heart, And lean not on your own understanding; In all your ways acknowledge Him, And He shall direct your paths." Mary grew as God stretched her faith. She let go of her fears, trusting that God would do what was best.

Let goods and kindred go,
This mortal life also;
The body they may kill:
God's truth abideth still,
His kindom is forever.[6]

PERSONAL REFLECTION

- In what ways have I allowed fears and "common sense," unsubmitted to God's will, to hinder His use of me?
- How have I impeded my spiritual growth by resting on what I have already done in service for Christ instead of pressing forward?
- What limits have I placed on God or people dear to me that I should surrender to God?

FURTHER READING Matthew 10:16–39

Williams, John. *A Narrative of Missionary Enterprises in the South Seas.* London: J. Snow, 1837.

DAY 17

FACING THINGS
AS THEY ARE

"It takes God to do anything anywhere."
—AMY CARMICHAEL, MISSIONARY TO JAPAN AND INDIA
(1867–1951)

*"But we have this treasure in earthen vessels, that the excellence
of the power may be of God and not of us."*
—2 CORINTHIANS 4:7

See! It is she! The child-stealing Amma! Run!"[1] The temple woman warned seven-year-old Pearl-Eyes as one of Amy Carmichael's local coworkers walked by. Pearl-Eyes looked up in hope, a new thought popping into her little head, "Maybe she could steal me!"

Not long before, Pearl-Eyes had run away from her guardians at one of the many Hindu temples in southern India. The little girl walked for three days over twenty miles to her hometown to find her mother, but the reunion was short-lived. The temple women tracked Pearl-Eyes down. Her mother, who had sold her to the temple as an infant, returned the girl to her captors.

"Don't you ever run away again!" the temple women scolded Pearl-Eyes. The little girl looked down at her hand, a burn scar reminding her of an earlier punishment. She wanted to flee again, but if her mother would not protect her, who would?

Then, Pearl-Eyes overheard two of the temple women whispering about her future. The child would soon be married to the god—tied to a hideous statue in the dark temple and dedicated for life as a temple prostitute. No doubt the girl did not fully understand all that she would face, but she bowed to the idol and cried pitifully, "Let me die! Oh, let me die!" When she heard of the "child-stealing Amma," she decided to run away once more. She had nothing to lose.

Carmichael's coworker found the desperate child at the empty Christian church and brought her to the Irish missionary's home. When Pearl-Eyes saw Carmichael sitting on her porch reading a book, the little girl ran to her and climbed into her lap.

"My name is Pearl-Eyes," she announced, "and I want to stay here always."[2] Carmichael was dubious. Who was this little girl? Was her story true?

Pearl-Eyes would be the first of many defenseless children Carmichael would rescue from the clutches of evil. Soon, Pickles, Tangles, and Imp would join Pearl-Eyes in Carmichael's growing family. God would turn Carmichael's ministry from itinerant evangelism to a children's shelter and orphanage. Upon hearing of children in danger, Carmichael would seek to rescue them from physical harm first. Then, by God's grace, she would help them find spiritual salvation through the gospel.

This story and others like it in Carmichael's 1903 book *Things As They Are* shocked the sensibilities of her Victorian readers.

Besides exposing little-publicized religious and cultural practices that harmed women and children, Carmichael also highlighted the daily grind of missions work. As the title suggests, she told things as they really were—the struggles, the setbacks, the small victories, and the daunting obstacles that stymied the missionaries' effectiveness. She took a stunningly direct approach for her times:

> We have tried to tell you the truth—the uninteresting, unromantic truth—about the heathen as we find them, the work as it is. More workers are needed. No words can tell how much they are needed, how much they are wanted here.
>
> But ... our business is to tell the truth. The work is not a pretty thing, to be looked at and admired. It is a fight. And battlefields are not beautiful.[3]

Missionaries of her generation tended to report only the successes, but Carmichael tempered expectations—her own and others'—with reality.[4]

Carmichael recounts an occasion when she had opportunity to share the gospel with a group of scholarly Hindu men. She comments, "I should like to finish up by saying, 'and several were converted,' but as yet that would not be true."[5] On another occasion, after telling of repeatedly being rebuffed in attempts to share the gospel, she explains, "The greatest difficulty of all in reaching the women is that they have no desire to be reached."[6] Throughout the world, this spiritual hardness continues to repel loving gospel advance.

Yet, Carmichael's goal with such candor was to increase prayer and recruit fresh laborers for the work in India.[7] She wanted her Christian readers to feel the darkness, recognize the futility without God's power, and join in the fight, forewarned and fore-armed by God's strength in this battle for souls.[8] Though the road is hard, God is there, and prayer is an essential weapon:

> Do you think we are writing like this because we are discouraged? No, we are not discouraged, except when sometimes we fear lest you should grow weary in prayer before the answer comes. This India is God's India. This work is His. Oh, join with us then, as we join with all our dear Indian brothers and sisters who are alive in the Lord, in waiting upon Him in that intensest [sic] form of waiting which waits on till the answer comes; join with us as we pray to the mighty God of revivals, "O Lord, revive Thy work! Revive Thy work in the midst of the years! In the midst of the years make known!" [Habakkuk 3:2][9]

Carmichael weaves rays of light around her dark descriptions. She points to God as the answer, saying, "Nothing is hopeless to God."[10] Yet, Carmichael writes, "It seems to us that it is more important that you should know about the reverses than about the successes of the [spiritual] war. We shall have all eternity to celebrate the victories, but we have only the few hours before sunset in which to win them."[11] There is still much to be done.

Today, we, too, need to understand things as they are—both where we live and on the mission field. We must tell the truth. We must present the whole picture, including both the successes and the struggles. Our social media posts, shared pictures, and even prayer requests often weave an artificial narrative instead of providing a balanced view of reality. We must not garnish a cow pie. If reality stinks, we must face it as it is. The truth is that hearts are hard, spiritual blindness is real, and setbacks are more numerous than successes. As Carmichael testified, the vast majority of the unreached prefer to stay that way. Even Jesus faced such apathy, prompting Him not to do His mighty works in some regions "because of their unbelief" (Matthew 13:58). The apostle Paul also was not shy describing the opposition he faced (2 Corinthians 11:23–30). Yet, among the difficulties, we should rejoice as we see God overcome the obstacles. The deliverance of Pearl-Eyes is one such gem of praise hidden among the gravel of destruction.

Take courage! "We have this treasure in earthen vessels," writes the apostle Paul, "that the excellency of the power may be of God, and not of us" (2 Corinthians 4:7). The same God that strengthened Carmichael to overcome the harsh realities of Indian ministry is the God with us today. As Carmichael observed, "It takes God to do anything anywhere."[12] Depend on Him!

PERSONAL REFLECTION

- What hard realities am I facing today?
- How can admitting the truth of these difficulties to others help me to depend more on God?
- What expectations do I have about the Christian life and serving God? Are these expectations true to reality and consistent with God's Word?

FURTHER READING   1 Corinthians 2

Carmichael, Amy. *Things As They Are: Mission Work in Southern India*. London: Morgan and Scott, 1905.

Elliot, Elisabeth. *A Chance to Die: The Life and Legacy of Amy Carmichael*. Old Tappan, NJ: Fleming H. Revell Company, 1987.

UNEXPECTED INFLUENCE

"The man who does not learn to wait upon the Lord and have his thoughts molded by Him will never possess that steady purpose and calm trust, which is essential to the exercise of wise influence upon others, in times of crisis and difficulty." [1]

—D. E. HOSTE, MISSIONARY TO CHINA (1861–1946)

"Wait on the Lord,
And keep His way,
And He shall exalt you."

—PSALM 37:34

F ew remembered D. E. Hoste—not with famous athletes C. T. Studd and Stanley Smith on the stage. Crowds across England and Scotland flocked to hear the Cambridge Seven. These young men had left promising futures to serve as missionaries with Hudson Taylor's China Inland Mission.[2] On February 4, 1885, the final night before they left for China, the departing missionary recruits spoke one last time.

Sandwiched between his famous companions, twenty-three-year-old D. E. Hoste rose to speak. Though he was the first of the Cambridge Seven to apply to the mission, Hoste knew he did not quite fit with the rest of the group. Of the seven, he was the only non-Cambridge alumnus. Instead, Hoste had been a lieutenant in the Royal Artillery. At his first interview with Hudson Taylor, the founder of the mission suggested the young man get more ministry experience. Therefore, Hoste volunteered in the decision room at D. L. Moody's revivals, leading men and women to Christ.[3] When the mission finally accepted Hoste, no one would have believed he would one day lead the mission.

Hoste stepped to the podium for his final address before heading to China. He briefly shared his testimony, asked for prayer, and took his seat. After the eloquence and energy of his companions, his quiet demeanor and high-pitched voice must have presented quite the contrast. Far away in India, Amy Carmichael would read a transcript of his few words and write, "Specially I was drawn in spirit to the one who had counted loss all that life as an officer of the Royal Artillery would have meant, and who had become a corn of wheat, willing to fall into the ground and die."[4] Her observation was the exception to the rule, as Hoste's more popular teammates continued to dominate the headlines.

In China, Hoste found himself once again overshadowed by his colleagues. He and Smith moved north to the Shanxi province. When Smith suggested that they needed to choose a leader for their mission team and then nominated himself, Hoste inwardly rebelled. Years afterward, he shared,

> When he put the matter thus bluntly to me, I was ruffled in my
> spirit. . . . Why should I serve under him? We were about the same

age, and had come to China together. Granted he was brilliant
with the language, could make easy contacts, and in other ways
was my superior, this did not seem sufficient reason to me. . . .
Later, on thinking over the situation, the Spirit of God probed
me, and I was forced to admit that I did not relish the thought of
being under my friend. I thought of my "face," what friends would
surmise, etc. The difficulty was in my own heart. It was impressed
upon me that unwillingness persisted in would mean my having
to part company with the Lord Jesus Christ, who dwells with
the humble ones, those who willingly go down, I therefore
accepted my friend's suggestion, and we worked happily together.
. . . I believe that crises like these, when we are tested as to our
willingness to go down, are the pivotal influences that shape our
destiny. Our subsequent ministry springs from the decisions we
make in these critical places.[5]

Hoste passed the spiritual test and served as Smith's faithful teammate for the next six months.

When Smith moved on to work in another city, Hoste again
submitted to work under someone else—this time the local
pastor Xi Shengmo. Though many of his European colleagues
criticized him for not asserting his authority as a foreign missionary, Hoste saw how the work prospered under Xi's leadership.
Furthermore, Hoste believed that only through local leaders
would the church become truly indigenous and lasting in Chinese
culture. Therefore, Hoste chose to work from the background in a
mentoring, training, and peacemaking role.[6]

During this time, God strengthened Hoste's spiritual walk.[7]
A junior missionary who boarded with Hoste in the early 1890s
described his host's devotional habits:

> He would close the large front doors and usually would spend some hours in intercessory prayer and Bible study. He usually prayed aloud, but in a very low tone, and would pace up and down the room while he was in prayer. . . . During his many journeys through the country to outlying villages and cities, he frequently sent his boy [whom he paid to assist him] ahead with the donkey and baggage for some distance, while he followed behind on foot, and prayed as he walked.[8]

The growth of Hoste's walk with God would prove critical to God's plan for his future.[9] On August 7, 1900, Taylor appointed Hoste to be his successor as head of the mission.[10] He would serve as general director for the next thirty-five years.

How did God prepare D. E. Hoste to lead? God chose the most forgettable of the Cambridge Seven. Hoste was neither the most talented nor the most intelligent of his peers. He served under both missionaries and local coworkers. The way up was the way down.

God used Hoste's experience and prayer life to lead the China Inland Mission into the second phase of its work. In forty years (1865–1905), the first phase had established gospel beachheads across inland China. With the bulk of the pioneering work finished, Hoste led the mission to grow these outposts into churches and Christian communities. Hoste's emphasis on indigenous principles—self-government, self-support, and self-propagation—would prepare the growing churches in China for the day when foreign missionaries would have to leave. By God's grace, the thousands of Chinese people the missionaries had led to Christ before 1950 would multiply into tens of millions by the late twentieth century.

Those who lead others must first learn to follow. God exhorts us: "Wait on the LORD, and keep His way, and He shall exalt you"

(Psalm 37:34). The desire to lead is not a sin (1 Timothy 3:1). However, the method for attaining that role often *is* sinful (3 John 9). God resists those who promote themselves, pushing their way into prominence (James 4:6). He exalts the humble (1 Peter 5:6).

Faithfully carry out the tasks God places before you. Be content to serve out of the limelight. Support the leaders God places over you. Draw close to God. Wait on Him. Keep His way. As Hoste attested, "Crises like these, when we are tested as to our willingness to go down, are the pivotal influences that shape our destiny." If God promotes you to leadership, remember the lessons you have learned. Lead boldly but with humility. Wield influence as Jesus did.

PERSONAL REFLECTION

- When others less qualified than me get promoted, what is my reaction?
- If I am unwilling to serve under others, what does that reveal about my submission to God?
- If someone lived in my home for one week and followed me everywhere I went, how would they describe my walk with God? Would they even notice my prayer life?

FURTHER READING 1 Peter 5:1–7

Thompson, Phyllis. *D. E. Hoste: A Prince with God.* London: China Inland Mission, 1949.

FULLY AND WHOLLY CONSECRATED

"The world has yet to see what God can do with and for and through a man who is fully and wholly consecrated to Him. . . . I'll be that man."

—D. L. MOODY, EVANGELISTIC PREACHER IN THE UNITED STATES AND THE UNITED KINGDOM (1837-1899)

"Blessed are those who . . . seek Him with the whole heart!"

—PSALM 119:2

Woodrow Wilson, future president of the United States, lay back in the barber's chair as a large, bearded man took the seat beside him. Decades later in 1914, Wilson still remembered this encounter with D. L. Moody:

> Every word that he [Moody] uttered, though it was not in the least didactic ["preachy"], showed a personal and vital interest in the man who was serving him; and before I got through with what was being done to me, I was aware that I had attended an

evangelistic service, because Mr. Moody was in the next chair. I purposely lingered in the room after he left, and noted the singular effect his visit had upon the barbers in that shop. They talked in undertones. They did not know his name, but they knew that something had elevated their thought. And I felt that I left that place as I should have left a place of worship.[1]

Such impromptu witnessing opportunities marked the life of D. L. Moody.

Moody, a shoe salesman turned preacher, promised God that he would share the gospel with one person per day as long as he lived. He would ask friend, acquaintance, and stranger alike the simple question: "Are you a Christian?" Early in his ministry in Chicago serving with the YMCA, his persistent enthusiasm for winning souls earned him the nickname "Crazy Moody."

In 1861, the American Civil War increased Moody's urgency to share the gospel. He left his YMCA work in Chicago temporarily to volunteer as a chaplain. Traveling across the Midwest to Union army camps, Moody daily faced the reality that the soldiers who heard his words stood on the brink of eternity. After the battles, Moody would see the corpses as he continued to share the gospel with the wounded survivors. Those pictures would linger in his mind long beyond the end of the war.

In 1872, Moody met a butcher turned evangelist named Henry Varley in Dublin, Ireland. After an all-night prayer meeting, Varley told him, "The world has yet to see what God can do with and for and through a man who is fully and wholly consecrated to Him." This brief statement moved Moody greatly: "A man! Varley meant any man. Varley didn't say he had to be educated, or brilliant, or anything else. Just a man. Well, by the Holy Spirit in me I'll be that man."[2] Just a few months later, Moody's ministry expanded exponentially.

As the crowds that came to hear him preach grew into the thousands, Moody never lost his focus on individuals. From 1873–1875, he held his first large evangelistic meetings in the United Kingdom. At the same time, he began training believers to lead individuals to Christ. After each service in auditoriums, warehouses, and churches across England and Scotland, Moody would invite those who wanted to believe on Christ to an after-meeting in what he called the "inquiry room." There, Moody, his songleader Ira Sankey, and a band of recruited "personal workers" would take their Bibles and lead people to Christ. Moody instructed the personal workers to be "patient and thorough dealing with each case, no hurrying from one to another. Wait patiently, and ply them with God's word, and think, oh! think, what it is to win a soul for Christ, and don't grudge the time spent on one person."[3] The crowds came to hear Moody, but Moody came to speak to individuals.

The people Moody led to the Lord and trained as personal workers soon spread across the world. The example Moody lived and the evangelistic methods he used went with them. Lilias Trotter attended Moody's training in London in 1875 and served as a personal worker in the inquiry rooms before the Lord led her to serve as a missionary in Africa.[4] Largely through Moody's influence in 1882–1883, the Lord raised up the Cambridge Seven, including C. T. Studd and D. E. Hoste, to join Hudson Taylor in China.[5] The Wordless Book, a simple evangelistic tool which Moody adapted from British pastor Charles Spurgeon, would travel with Trotter to Africa, Gilmour to Mongolia, and Taylor to China. Moody's efforts to train young men and women sent many into missions across the world through the Moody Bible Institute and in other universities through the Student Volunteer Movement which he helped to launch.[6]

Despite Moody's astounding success in the United Kingdom and the United States, the preacher humbly pointed to the power of prayer and to the Holy Spirit as the source of these results. He once said, "I know perfectly well that wherever I go and preach, there are many better preachers known and heard than I am; all that I can say about it is that the Lord uses me."[7] On another occasion, Moody attested, "Any power I have comes from the Spirit of God."[8] From early on in his Chicago ministry, he established daily prayer meetings. He wrote to his mother: "I have been to prayer meetings every night but two for eight months."[9] In addition, Moody established prayer meetings in concert with his evangelistic meetings wherever he traveled. Often the noon prayer meeting Moody initiated continued long after he had left.[10] Furthermore, he himself spent much time in private prayer alone and with his coworkers. Moody became a notable example of dedication and dependence on God.

Few believers today respond to God's call for surrender like Moody did. Yet, God encourages each individual, "Blessed are those who keep His testimonies, Who seek Him with the whole heart" (Psalm 119:2). Our Creator and Savior commands all believers to fully and wholly consecrate their lives to Him: "I beseech you therefore, brethren, by the mercies of God, that you present your bodies a living sacrifice, holy, acceptable to God, which is your reasonable service" (Romans 12:1). When you consider Jesus' sacrifice for us on the cross, the kind of passion for

God and concern for individual souls that Moody exhibited just makes sense (2 Corinthians 5:14–15). Do you dare to show the world what God would do with and for and through a fully and wholly consecrated you?

PERSONAL REFLECTION

- What is hindering me from total commitment to Christ today? Why am I content to live short of full consecration to God?
- When is the last time I shared the gospel or led someone to the Lord? Could I endeavor to share the gospel or hand out a tract at least once every day?
- What would help me show more interest in the individuals around me today?

FURTHER READING   Psalm 119:1–10

Pollock, John. *D. L. Moody: Moody Without Sankey.* Fearn, Ross-shire, Scotland: Christian Focus Publications, 1997.

OVERCOMING BY LOVE, PRAYER, AND SACRIFICE

"The conquest of the Holy Land should be attempted in no other way than . . . by love, by prayer, by tears and the offering of our own lives."

—RAYMOND LULL, MISSIONARY TO TUNISIA AND ALGERIA (C. 1232–1315)

"And they overcame him by the blood of the Lamb and by the word of their testimony, and they did not love their lives to the death."

—REVELATION 12:11

Wave after wave of European kings, knights, and foot soldiers poured into the Middle East between 1094 and Raymond Lull's birth in 1232. They answered the call of both monarchs and Roman Catholic priests to destroy the Muslims who had spread across the land of Israel and crept toward southern Europe.[1] In the wake of the Seventh Crusade (1248–1254),

Lull, a Catalonian Spanish merchant from Mallorca in the Mediterranean Sea, pleaded for a new approach to confronting the Muslims—love, prayer, and sacrifice.

Daring to contradict both the despotic popes and popular European opinion, Lull wrote, "I see many knights going to the Holy Land beyond the seas and thinking that they can acquire it by force of arms; but in the end all are destroyed before they attain that which they think to have."[2] He continued in prayer: "It is my belief, O Christ, that the conquest of the Holy Land should be attempted in no other way than Thou and Thy apostles undertook to accomplish it, by love, by prayer, by tears and the offering of our own lives."[3] What a revolutionary idea for his day![4]

These were no mere words. After his conversion from a life of debauchery in July 1266, thirty-four-year-old Lull found a new purpose. He determined to share Christ's love with the Muslim peoples that his father's generation had fought to drive from southern Spain. To prepare for this mission, Lull disappeared into his study for nine years.[5] Biographer Samuel Zwemer reports that "besides his Arabic studies, Lull spent these nine years in spiritual meditation, in what he calls 'contemplating God.'"[6] Then, he studied Islam and developed his own philosophical system to combat Muslim ideas with Christian truth. In addition, Lull sought to recruit missionaries for the Middle East, even vainly petitioning popes for this cause.[7]

In 1291 when the pope showed more interest in another bloody crusade than a missionary campaign, Lull launched out on his own for the northern coast of Africa. The fifty-six-year-old scholar loaded a library of books onto a ship headed for Tunisia. Then his courage failed him, and he and his library fled before the ship left Genoa, Italy. Lull felt the weight of the risk. The theological and moral bankruptcy of the Roman Catholic Church was not the only reason no one else had attempted to take the gospel to the Muslims.

No sooner had the ship left the harbor without him than Lull regretted his decision. With renewed determination, Lull boarded another ship some weeks later. When he finally arrived in Tunis, the European Christian announced an open debate between himself and the intellectuals of the city to argue the validity of Christianity and Islam. The scholars accepted his offer. After a couple of debates, the local authorities grew alarmed by Lull's arguments against Islam and the small group of locals who had defected to Christianity. The sultan arrested Lull and locked him in a dungeon.

Before he could be executed, another Muslim leader convinced the sultan to change the sentence to banishment from Tunisia. With a threat of stoning if he ever returned, the authorities put Lull on a ship bound for Europe. Undaunted, Lull slipped away before the vessel left the port. He stubbornly remained in Tunis for another three months, secretly discipling his flock of new believers.

In 1307 after missionary journeys in Cyprus, Syria, and Armenia, seventy-five-year-old Lull dared to return to northern Africa, this time to the Algerian town of Bugia. With reckless boldness, Lull once again proclaimed a public debate with Muslim scholars. An enraged mob ended the debate prematurely. A high-ranking Muslim cleric managed to restrain the crowd from killing Lull on the spot, but he could not understand how Lull could put himself in such danger. Lull replied, "Death has no terrors whatever for a sincere servant of Christ who is laboring to bring souls to a knowledge of the truth."[8] Such audacity got Lull locked away for the next six months.

While the aging missionary languished in prison, his captors endeavored to entice him to embrace Islam. Rather than convince him through arguments on the merits of their religion, they attempted to seduce him with women, wealth, and prestige.[9] When these temptations proved useless, his captors once again decided to banish rather than execute the elderly preacher.

On August 14, 1314, Lull, now eighty-two years old, launched one last missionary journey into Muslim lands.[10] He would once more attempt to win Muslims to Christ through the love he shared and lived among them. As Lull often said, "He who loves not lives not; he who lives by the Life can not die."[11] Love for Christ and the Muslims for whom Christ died motivated Lull.

Upon his return to Algeria, Lull for once avoided the spotlight of public debate. For ten months, the old man quietly shepherded the believers he had led to Christ in his previous visit. He prayed. He loved. He shared the gospel.

Then, on June 30, 1315, Lull could hold himself back no longer. He emerged from secrecy into the public square, preaching Christ before all with no regard for personal safety. As happened to Stephen in Acts 8, an angry mob dragged Lull out of the city and stoned him to death.

How did Lull have such boldness and confidence? First, Lull evidenced faith in Christ's death and resurrection. Since Christ arose, Lull knew he, too, would one day rise. Second, Lull emphasized the importance of prayer and devotion to Christ. Like Moses' forty years in the wilderness, God used Lull's lengthy

Arabic studies as time alone to grow him in his faith. Throughout his life, Lull composed hymns and wrote sixty-two books of meditation and devotion.[12]

How do we reach the Muslim world? Today, the carnage of the Crusades has been replaced by blasts of terrorism and retaliatory invasions. The lands of Islam seem as impossible to reach as they did in Lull's day seven hundred years ago. Yet, Muslims and their large families have immigrated across the world. Whether they be in the Middle East or next door, how do we reach these dear souls for whom Christ died? By acts of love, prayers of dependence, and willingness to sacrifice. Love breaks down barriers and casts out fear. The sacrificial love of Christ compels us and convinces others (2 Corinthians 5:14–21). The love of genuine Christians must overcome the aggression of secular Christendom (John 13:35). Let us win Muslims to the truth of the gospel as Lull urged—"by love, by prayer, by tears and the offering of our own lives."

PERSONAL REFLECTION

- How can my life better reflect the love of Christ to those who see Him as an enemy?
- What keeps me from offering my own life for the cause of Christ and the salvation of those in darkness?
- Is my love for Christ greater than my fear of danger, suffering, or ridicule?

FURTHER READING   Matthew 5:43–48

Zwemer, Samuel M. *Raymond Lull: First Missionary to the Muslims*. New York: Funk and Wagnalls, 1902.

WORK AND WAIT

"We dare not rest; but by prayer and supplication and labours oft, we must wrestle and struggle and patiently wait and look for the promised blessing." [1]

—JAMES CHALMERS, MISSIONARY TO POLYNESIA AND NEW GUINEA (1841–1901)

"Wait on the Lord;
Be of good courage,
And He shall strengthen your heart;
Wait, I say, on the Lord!"

—PSALM 27:14

What are they saying?" James Chalmers asked his Papuan companion. Two bands of cannibal tribesmen had been following them through the jungles of New Guinea all day.

"They are saying they intend to kill us. Let us kneel down and pray." [2]

"No, no!" Chalmers exclaimed. "Let us walk and pray."

Depending on God for protection, Chalmers boldly marched ahead. Once again, God spared the missionary's life. For Chalmers, trusting God and cheating death had become a way of life.

As a youth in Scotland, Chalmers nearly drowned three times. This prompted his father to say, "Eh, laddie . . . I'm sure ye'll nae [never] be drowned."[3] Chalmers would survive shipwreck four times during his life.

Yet to Chalmers, depraved men presented a greater danger than the sea. He got his first glimpse of sin's dehumanizing effects in his home country while serving in an inner-city rescue mission. He would later tell a friend that "apart from its cannibalism, even New Guinea presented no sights more terrible for degradation and impurity than Glasgow."[4] The Lord was preparing Chalmers for his future work.

When Chalmers journeyed in 1866 as a new missionary to Rarotonga in the Cook Islands, he once again confronted the depravity of man. He and his wife sailed from England aboard the *John Williams*, a ship owned by the London Mission Society. However, the storm-battered vessel foundered before it reached Samoa. Stranded in the middle of the Pacific Ocean, Chalmers and his wife had no choice but to complete their journey aboard the only ship available—a pirate ship. Its American captain, the notorious Bully Hayes, was known for swindling, kidnapping, rape, and murder.

Undaunted, Chalmers preached the gospel to the pirate. Despite Hayes' reputation, the pirate allowed Chalmers to hold church services on his ship. Chalmers' influence caused Hayes to say, "If only you were near me, I should certainly become a new man, and lead a different life."[5] However, Hayes did not believe the gospel and did not become a new man. A few days after Chalmers disembarked, the pirate once again attempted to murder one of his sailors.

When Chalmers landed in Rarotonga, he found that the late missionary John Williams and his followers had made great progress in winning men and women to Christ. Though the society was still plagued by drunkenness and promiscuity, the island was not the pioneer field Chalmers had expected. He wrote,

> For years I had longed to get amongst real heathen and savages, and I was disappointed when we landed on Rarotonga and found them so much civilized and Christianized. I wrote to the Directors at Blomfield Street [LMS headquarters], stating my disappointment, and begged them to appoint us to Espiritu Santo in the New Hebrides [an unreached island in modern-day Vanuatu, near the islands where his contemporary John Paton ministered].[6]

Chalmers longed to spearhead a gospel advance where no missionary had gone before.

Just over a decade later, Chalmers got his chance to launch a pioneer work among the cannibals of New Guinea. Long before Russell and Darlene Deibler, Stanley Dale, or Don Richardson took the gospel to these long-forgotten tribesmen, Chalmers and a handful of Rarotongan believers risked their lives in the uncharted mountains of the island. Chalmers' daring exploits earned him the title of "the Livingstone of New Guinea."[7] As a youth, Chalmers had read about David Livingstone's pioneer journeys into central Africa.[8] As an adult, Chalmers in New Guinea imitated Livingstone's work and published books about what he found. In 1886, the Royal Geographical Society awarded Chalmers the same diploma they had given Livingstone.[9]

In 1890, Chalmers met renowned author Robert Louis Stevenson on board a ship from Sydney to Samoa. The atheist author and the missionary struck up a lasting friendship. Stevenson even remarked in a letter to Chalmers, "If I had met you when I was a boy and a bachelor, how different my life would have been!"[10] In admiration, Stevenson began calling Chalmers "the Great Heart of New Guinea."[11] Through Chalmers' writings, explorations, and contact with notable people of his day, the pioneer missionary's reputation grew.

Yet, fame does not protect a missionary from hungry cannibals. Chalmers endured frequent threats on his life as he pressed on in New Guinea. Gradually, in regions where he and his local coworkers spread the gospel, the ovens that had cooked the flesh of humans went permanently cold.[12] However, Chalmers always pushed forward, walking and praying into unreached areas of the island.[13] He described his goals early in his Papuan ministry:

> Christ's glory and man's eternal good are all we seek. Oh, that we saw all on this island Christ's; and until we do, we dare not rest; but by prayer and supplication and labours oft, we must wrestle and struggle and patiently wait and look for the promised blessing.[14]

Such focus shaped Chalmers' life.

Chalmers' example provides believers today with a vivid picture of waiting on God. Earlier in his life, Chalmers waited and worked in Glasgow while preparing for the mission field. He waited and worked for ten years in Rarotonga while hoping to be sent to a pioneer field. Chalmers waited on God as he worked in

New Guinea, trusting God to protect him and further the gospel despite the depravity surrounding him.

Waiting on God does not mean inaction. Waiting on God is readiness to jump into action when God opens a door because your eyes are already on Him (2 Chronicles 20:12). It is faithfully doing what God has placed before you as you eagerly look for the next step in your service to Christ. Waiting on God is the attitude of dependence, trusting God to do what only He can do as you do what He has commanded. Isaiah 64:4 promises, "For since the beginning of the world Men have not heard nor perceived by the ear, Nor has the eye seen any God besides You, Who acts for the one who waits for Him." Work as you wait, knowing God will be true to His promises.

Chalmers charged forward until the very end. He knew when to "walk and pray," avoiding danger. Yet, even as he neared his sixtieth birthday, he did not shy away from risk. On April 8, 1901, the day after Easter, Chalmers, young missionary Oliver Tomkins, and a small team of Polynesian coworkers dared to enter yet another new territory with the gospel—Goaribari Island. Along the Aird River near the aptly named Risk Point, the depravity of man once again reared its ugly head. Tribesmen invited the missionary team into their village and then savagely turned on them, massacring and feasting on them all.

Yet even in Chalmers' death, God was at work. The news of the missionary explorer's martyrdom rocked the world.[15] Within a year of his death, authors in the U.S. and England published two biographies of Chalmers. Christians surrendered to step into his place. Ruatoka, one of Chalmers' Papuan coworkers, wrote after his death,

Hear my wish. It is a great wish. The remainder of my strength I would spend in the place where Tamate [Chalmers] and Mr. Tomkins were killed. In that village I would live. In that place where they killed men, Jesus Christ's name and His word I would teach to the people, that they may become Jesus's children. My wish is just this. You know it. I have spoken.[16]

Though God took Chalmers to his final rest, the efforts to reach New Guinea "for Christ's glory and man's eternal good" did not end with his death. Local believers and new missionaries rose up to continue what Chalmers had begun.

PERSONAL REFLECTION

- Do I tend to work without waiting on the Lord? How?
- Do I tend to wait on the Lord without working in the meantime? Why?
- What are two things I can do today while waiting on the Lord to work?

FURTHER READING Psalm 27

Lovett, Richard. *James Chalmers: His Autobiography and Letters.* New York: Fleming H. Revell, 1902.

DAY 22

SAVE ME
FROM MYSELF

"I prayed that God would show me what to do
and deliver me—and He did."

—GLADYS AYLWARD, MISSIONARY TO CHINA (1902–1970)

"Help me, O Lord my God!
Oh, save me according to Your mercy,
That they may know that this is Your hand—
That You, Lord, have done it!"

—PSALM 109:26–27

A piercing wind chattered the teeth of thirty-year-old Gladys Aylward. The four-foot, ten-inch woman perched atop her luggage on a deserted platform of the Trans-Siberian railway on October 24, 1932. From this station near the Manchurian border in the Soviet Union, Aylward could hear gunshots echoing through the forest as the Russian and Japanese armies exchanged fire. The train would go no further toward the war zone. As Aylward watched the snow swirl through the night sky, she wondered how

God would get her to Tianjin, China, where elderly missionary Jeannie Lawson waited for the young woman to join her work. Alone in this desolate place, Aylward turned to God. She later wrote of that day: "I prayed that God would show me what to do and deliver me—and He did." [1] How did Gladys Aylward find herself in this predicament?

In 1916 when she was only fourteen years old, Aylward entered the workforce as a maid in a wealthy British home, but she dreamed of becoming an actress. Despite her Christian upbringing, she had no hunger for spiritual things until she attended an evangelistic meeting in 1920. After she trusted Christ as her Savior, the young maid's interests soon turned from the theater to Christian service. She began volunteering at her local church, with the Young Life Campaign, and in a rescue mission for the poor.

During this time, Aylward came across a magazine article about China. The needs of millions without Christ tugged at her heart. Who would take the gospel to them? She began asking her friends and relatives if they would go, but no one showed any interest. Finally, she decided that if no one else would go, then she would. She later said,

> I wasn't God's first choice for what I've done for China. . . . I don't know who it was. . . . It must have been a man . . . a well-educated man. I don't know what happened. Perhaps he died. Perhaps he wasn't willing . . . and God looked down . . . and saw Gladys Aylward . . . And God said, "Well, she's willing." [2]

Only too aware of her lack of qualifications, she applied to Hudson Taylor's China Inland Mission.

After three months of initial training and assessment in 1930, the China Inland Mission rejected her candidacy. This working-class maid had neither the background, the education, nor the language aptitude to survive the rigors of China. As she left her exit interview, the chairman asked her, "What are you going to do, Miss Aylward?"

"I don't know," she replied, "but I am sure God does not want me to be a parlormaid again. He wants me to do something for Him."[3]

Nevertheless, since Aylward did not have immediate plans, the chairman offered her a job as a housekeeper for a couple of retired missionaries in Bristol. Aylward took the position, though regretful that her time of missionary training had come to an end: "I'm sorry I haven't been able to learn much at the [China Inland Mission] college," she told the chairman, "but I *have* learned to pray, *really* pray as I never did before, and that is something for which I'll always be grateful."[4] And pray she did.

Every day, Aylward prayed and read the Word of God. She meditated on the biblical accounts of Abraham, Moses, and Nehemiah. She asked herself, "Gladys Aylward, is Nehemiah's God your God?"[5] As she observed the faith of her retired missionary employers, her burden for China only grew.

After two years, Aylward decided she could wait no longer. She gathered her most precious belongings and prayed: "O God, here's the Bible about which I long to tell others, here's my *Daily Light* that every day will give me a new promise, and here is 2½d [$0.20 USD]. If you want me, I am going to China with these."[6] Whether or not she had sufficient funds or the sponsorship of a mission board, Aylward chose to step into the unknown. Going alone to China was daring, but was it wise? Where is the line between godly boldness and foolish presumption?

As she prepared for her journey, Aylward heard about seventy-three-year-old Jeannie Lawson, a veteran missionary who had recently returned to China. Lawson needed an assistant, and Aylward saw the hand of God in this opportunity. Her parents helped her pack her bags, and with Lawson awaiting her arrival, Aylward took the least expensive route from England to Tianjin, China—overland by train through northern Europe and war-torn Asia.[7]

After a long hike through the snow from that lonely Siberian train station, Aylward barely escaped the clutches of corrupt Russian officials. At the port city of Vladivostok, God answered her prayers, and a sympathetic Russian woman helped her slip onto a Japanese ship and away from the war. After a stop in Japan, Aylward finally reached her destination.

Aylward's daring exploits over the next seventeen years in north-central China would become legendary.[8] Her gospel work involved everything from evangelistic meetings in a rustic hotel among working-class muleteers, to traveling across the countryside as an agent of the provincial government to unbind Chinese women's feet, to rescuing orphans during the Sino-Japanese War. Despite the China Inland Mission's assessment, Aylward learned to speak Mandarin Chinese so well that when she adopted the dress and customs of the region, many locals assumed she was Chinese. Only God could take a parlor maid who trusted Him and use her in such astounding ways.

What gave Aylward the courage to step into such daunting circumstances to serve the Lord? As a working-class woman of that era, she had few opportunities to prepare for missions work. Despite this disadvantage, Aylward believed God was God and relied wholly on Him. Her weapons were the Word of God and its promises. Her defense, when obstacles arose, was prayer. Yes, her naivety occasionally endangered her life. Sometimes her prayers for deliverance were pleas for God to rescue her from herself. In addition, her methods at times exposed her lack of biblical training.[9] Regardless, Aylward used what opportunities and skills she did have beyond all expectations. When others she knew were unwilling to serve in China, she launched out, relying on no support except for her relationship with God.

God delights in overturning expectations to accomplish His work in the world. He seeks out unworthy but willing servants who rely on Him. Whether you blunder into difficulty or danger overtakes you despite your precautions, God hears the prayer of His servant: "Help me, O Lord my God! Oh, save me according to Your mercy, That they may know that this is Your hand—That You, Lord, have done it" (Psalm 109:26–27)! Yes, you should pursue biblical training, sharpen your ministry skills, listen to wise counsel, and research the best methods. However, the time will come when, regardless of how prepared you are, you must step into the unknown, trusting God and His promises. When God works as only He can to preserve you, sustain you, and use you to accomplish the improbable, He alone gets the glory.

PERSONAL REFLECTION

- On what relationships do I rely more than my relationship with God?
- What am I allowing to limit my expectations of how God could use me?
- In what ways do I need God to save me from myself? How can I remedy these deficiencies to better serve God and others?

FURTHER READING   Psalm 109:21–31

BOLDNESS FROM BEING WITH JESUS

"In the vast plain to the north I have sometimes seen, in the morning sun, the smoke of a thousand villages where no missionary has ever been."

—ROBERT MOFFAT, MISSIONARY TO NAMIBIA AND SOUTH AFRICA (1795–1883)

"Now when they saw the boldness ... they marveled. And they realized that they had been with Jesus."

—ACTS 4:13

Drive your spears to my heart," shouted twenty-seven-year-old Robert Moffat as he peeled back his waistcoat. "When you have slain me, my companions will know that the hour has come for them to depart." A mob had gathered at the Moffats' door, threatening to expel the young missionaries from their post in Kuruman, South Africa.

Since the Moffats had arrived in Kuruman in May 1821 two years earlier, drought had stricken the north-central region of the country. When the native rainmakers could not coax water from the sky, the locals blamed the newcomers, their chapel bell, and even a bag of salt that Moffat had brought in the wagon that he had been repairing when the mob arrived. Mary Moffat, holding their infant daughter, stood at the door, fearing what the angry villagers might do to her daring husband.

"These men must have ten lives, when they are so fearless of death," grunted one leader as the crowd dispersed. "There must be something in immortality."[1] Though none of the Tswana people had as yet responded to the gospel, they had begun to recognize that Moffat's testimony reinforced what he taught about eternal life.

Moffat prized eternal souls more than he valued his own life. Originally, he had trained to risk his life for the gospel's sake in the South Pacific. He and John Williams had prepared together before the leaders of their mission sent Moffat to the southern tip of Africa. No matter his listeners' ethnicity, Moffat longed to lead lost souls to the Savior. In a letter to his parents before sailing for Africa in early 1817, he wrote, "Oh that I had a thousand lives, and a thousand bodies; all of them should be devoted to no other employment but to preach Christ to these degraded, despised, yet beloved mortals."[2] This burden had only grown in the five years since his appointment.

Yet, early on as a single man in a remote post near Warmbad (just over the modern-day South African border with Namibia), Moffat struggled with his calling and with the fruitlessness of his work. He later described how God sustained him:

> I was wont to pour out my soul among the granite rocks
> surrounding this station, now in sorrow, and then in joy; and
> more than once I have taken my violin . . . and, reclining upon
> one of the huge masses, have, in the stillness of the evening,
> played and sung."[3]

Moffat looked to God, and God encouraged his heart.

Moffat began learning to rely on Christ as a youth. When he first left his home in Scotland for a gardening job down south in England, his mother begged him to promise that he would read his Bible daily. When Moffat protested that he did read his Bible, his mother replied, "I know you do, but you do not read it regularly. . . . O Robert, my son, read much in the New Testament. Read much in the Gospels—the blessed Gospels; then you cannot well go astray. If you pray, the Lord Himself will teach you."[4] Moffat gave his word and later said, "I never forgot my promise to my mother."[5] His mother also planted the first seeds of his future work, reading to him of Moravian missionaries in Greenland and India.

With this spiritual foundation, the Lord grew Moffat's perseverance and boldness. The confrontation at his Kuruman home in 1822 was not the first danger he faced. In January 1818, the not yet married Moffat had ventured into modern-day Namibia, the domain of the feared Oorlam chief, Jager Afrikaner.[6] This outlaw and his band of raiders had left a path of thievery and destruction, attacking indigenous villagers and colonials alike. The countryside had allied against him. When Moffat announced his intention of venturing into Afrikaner's territory, the Dutch settlers nearby pitied the naive young man. Soon after his departure, rumors spread of Moffat's demise.

When he emerged with a new companion some months later, a Dutch farmer and his wife were convinced that Moffat was a ghost. In fear, the farmer cried out, "Don't come near me. . . . You have been long since murdered by Africaner [sic]. Everybody says you were murdered, and a man told me he had seen your bones."[7] When Moffat laughed and said that Afrikaner was, in fact, his friend, the farmer protested that this was more impossible than the missionary's survival! Turning to his traveling companion he had not yet introduced, Moffat said, "This, then, is Africaner [sic]."[8] The missionary and this new believer were traveling together to seek a pardon in Cape Town. What amazing grace for God to save and transform such a violent chief!

For over fifty years, Moffat boldly served the Lord in South Africa. He braved the dangers of war, desert, lions, hippopotamuses, and cobras. He endured through ten years of seeming fruitlessness. He persevered for over thirty years to learn the Tswana language, reduce it to writing, and then translate the entire Bible into it. In publishing the Scriptures and establishing his mission base at Kuruman, Moffat laid the foundation for outreach into regions beyond. As he recruited missionaries, including his future son-in-law David Livingstone, he told them, "In the vast plain to the north I have sometimes seen, in the morning sun, the smoke of a thousand villages where no missionary has ever been."[9] He accomplished much, yet there was so much more to be done.

Even today, the work of God around the globe looms large. Those who have gone before us have done a lion's share, yet the population of the world has exploded since they passed into glory. Where missionaries have previously gone, missionaries must go once again. The land is the same, but the population is different. The smoke of a thousand villages has been replaced by the blink of a million smart phones. The glow of those screens illuminates faces that need the true light of the gospel. Where can we find the courage to meet this glaring need?

Speaking to a group of children in England in 1840, Moffat pointed to the source of motivation and strength for the daunting task of world missions:

> There may be here a [Robert] Morrison—there may be here a [John] Williams—there may be here a [William] Carey—there may be here a [William] Milne—there may be here a [Thomas] Coke—there may be here a [John] Wesley—there may be here a [George] Whitefield—there may be here a John Knox for aught I know, for the world requires reformers yet. O, the field is great; there is a call for missionaries, and for missionary effort. Let me hope that many here, boys and girls, will become men and women—missionaries and missionaries' wives, to go out perhaps to Africa. You may come there and cast your eyes perhaps on a mound of stones that covers the remains of Robert Moffat, who is now addressing you. You will remember his words—you will remember his last entreaty, his last wish—read your Bibles, read your Bibles.[10]

Your time with God in His Word is the launchpad for future service for Him.

What can give you boldness and perseverance in the face of the impossibilities of the Great Commission? Know your God, and spend time with Jesus. Daniel 11:32 states, "The people who know their God shall be strong, and carry out great exploits." Acts 4:13 sheds further light on this key to boldness: "Now when they [the anti-Christian religious leaders] saw the boldness of Peter and John, and perceived that they were uneducated and untrained men, they marveled. And they realized that they had been with Jesus." Be with Jesus. Communicate with Him constantly. Open your heart to God's leading through His Word. As Moffat simply pleaded, "Read your Bibles."

PERSONAL REFLECTION

- How consistently do I spend quality time with God, praying and meditating on His Word?
- In what areas do I need to be bolder regardless of my personality type?
- How does my level of boldness for Christ reflect on how truly I trust God's promises?

FURTHER READING   Acts 5:17–32

Deane, David J. *Robert Moffat: The Missionary Hero of Kuruman.* New York: Fleming H. Revell, 1880.

DAY 24

CONTAGIOUS TRUST

"We may not live to see it, but the awakening will come, as surely as the sun will rise tomorrow." [1]
—MARY MOFFAT, MISSIONARY TO SOUTH AFRICA (1795–1871)

"Who, contrary to hope, in hope believed."
—ROMANS 4:18

S end us a communion service, we shall want it some day," wrote Mary Moffat from South Africa in 1827.[2] Her friend in England wished to send the missionary wife something for their work. For eight years in Kuruman, there had been no need for communion cups and plates because the villagers showed no interest in the gospel. What Mary had written in August 1822 remained true: "We have no prosperity in the work, not the least sign of good being done. The Tswana villagers seem more careless [disinterested] than ever, and seldom enter the church." Her husband Robert's letters conveyed the same theme: "They turn a deaf ear to the voice of love, and treat with scorn the glorious doctrines of salvation."[3] Yet, Mary ordered a communion set in faith that the Lord's Supper would one day be celebrated among the Tswana people.[4]

Two years later, Mary and her husband marked their ten-year anniversary laboring among the Tswana. Hearts remained indifferent to the gospel, and the communion dishes had not yet made the lengthy journey by ship and oxcart to Kuruman. Then, with no apparent cause beyond the Moffats' faithful witness and persistent prayers, God's Spirit began to work. Hard hearts softened. Tears flowed over the state of their souls. Men and women turned to Christ for salvation. In May 1829, the first twelve locals followed the Lord in baptism, and when they observed the Lord's Supper for the first time, the long-awaited communion set arrived just in time for the service.

From her childhood in the first decade of the 1800s, Mary began to learn to walk by faith. She attended a Moravian school where she heard of missionaries that had first landed in South Africa in 1737. She prayed that God would send her there. As she entered adulthood, her passion for serving God grew. When she sensed a similar heart in her father's young gardener, Mary fell in love with him.

The gardener, Robert Moffat, was awaiting approval by the London Missionary Society to serve overseas. However, two difficulties lay in Mary's path. First, Moffat was headed for the South Pacific, not South Africa. Second, her parents refused to consent to their marriage. God quickly resolved the first apparent issue when the London Missionary Society asked Moffat to go to South Africa, but three years of separation and prayer intervened before God changed her parents' hearts.

On September 7, 1819, twenty-four-year-old Mary sailed alone to join Moffat in South Africa. An overjoyed Robert exulted in God's answer to their prayers, writing to his parents:

> I have just received letters from Miss Smith [the future Mary Moffat]. The whole scene is changed. I have now reason to believe that God will make her path plain to Africa. This, I trust, will be soon, for a missionary without a wife in this country is like a boat with one oar.[5]

Mary would not be just a second oar. She would become a second engine in their work together at Kuruman.

Yet, while the Moffats' marriage blossomed, the work withered. When Robert grew discouraged, Mary prayed, analyzed their efforts, and encouraged her husband. When Robert lamented, "Think, my dear, how long we have been preaching to this people, and no fruit yet appears," Mary replied with great insight,

> The gospel has not yet been preached to them in their own tongue in which they were born. They have heard it only through interpreters, and interpreters who have themselves no just understanding, no real love of the truth. We must not expect the blessing till you are able, from your own lips and in their language, to bring it through their ears into their hearts.

Her husband took her words to heart, saying, "From that hour, I gave myself with untiring diligence to the acquisition of the language."[6] Mary's contagious trust in God reinvigorated Robert's faith in God.

With Mary's full support and selfless sacrifice, Robert took long treks into villages far from the English- and Dutch-speaking cities to fully immerse himself in the Tswana language and to continue his attempts to spread the gospel. Moffat would later testify, "I can tell you she has often sent me away from house and home for months together for evangelising purposes, and in my absence has managed the station as well, or better than I could have done it myself."[7] Better yet, Mary stoked the fires of her husband's hope in God, saying, "We may not live to see it, but the awakening will come, as surely as the sun will rise tomorrow."[8] God let them live to see it.

At their home base in Kuruman, Mary prayed and worked. She cared for their growing family, including her ten children and a couple of adopted orphans.[9] She taught local women and children the Word of God. She opened a school to train women to sew their own clothes. When lions stalked her husband in the wilderness and hippopotamuses threatened his river crossings, Mary prayed for his safety.[10] When enemies threatened the road Robert traveled to return home, God heard her prayers and ended a friendly chief's elephant hunt early so he would accompany Robert back to their home. Though she often faced dangers of war, disease, and drought, Mary found Robert's reassurance to her parents in England to be true: "She is under the care of our ever-present God, and united to one who promises to be father, mother, and husband to her."[11] Her steadfast faith inspired her husband.

In 1870, old age forced the Moffats to retire in England.[12] Many praised Robert for his accomplishments over nearly sixty years in South Africa. However, their son John said, "My father never would have been the missionary he was but for her care."[13] When Mary passed away about a year after their return to England, her final words were a prayer for her husband. Robert reminisced,

"For fifty-three years I have had her to pray for me."[14] Mary's unceasing prayers, tireless labor, and optimistic faith bolstered her husband's resolve and furthered the evangelization of southern Africa.

Romans 4:18 tells of Abraham, who like Mary Moffat, "contrary to hope, in hope believed" because he trusted God's promise. Abraham's faith led him to follow God into the unknown, and his wife Sarah's faith gave her strength to follow her husband. Encouraging each other through triumph and weakness, they navigated the minefield of life. The faith of both husband and wife is cataloged in Hebrews 11, inspiring generations to persevere.

Cultivate a contagious faith. May your walk with God uplift you and those around you. May your hope in God overcome rather than succumb to the discouragement that strikes when fruit is meager and obstacles many. May God use you to quietly inspire others to keep on.

PERSONAL REFLECTION

- If married, what kind of spiritual influence do I have on my spouse?
- If not married, how high on my list of requirements for a future spouse is their spiritual life?
- What are three ways I can encourage my pastor or the believers in my local church?

FURTHER READING   **Hebrews 11:8–13**

Brain, Belle Marvel, and David Hosaflook. *Love Stories of Great Missionaries*. Albania: Institute for Albanian and Protestant Studies, 2021.[15]

WALK IN THE DARK WITH GOD

"I am willing to walk in the dark with God."

—XI SHENGMO, PREACHER IN CHINA (C. 1836–1896)

"Put on the whole armor of God, that you may be able to stand against the wiles of the devil. . . . praying always with all prayer and supplication in the Spirit."

—EPHESIANS 6:11–18

Xi Zizhi stumbled and fell into his bed, overcome once again by opium.[1] The addiction had destroyed his once-illustrious career as a Confucian scholar and community leader in the Shanxi province. There was no escape for him or for many of his countrymen across China. Fields surrounding his village once staved off famine through their produce. Now, they flowered with poppies to meet the demand of the addicts and those who profited from them.[2] The local population joked that eleven people out of ten smoked opium.[3] At age forty-three, Xi was one of the helpless addicts.

Then, the advertisement came. Xi was suspicious. A foreigner in a neighboring village had sponsored an essay contest. Xi's friends all agreed that he was the man to win the cash prize. Xi examined the criteria for the essays. The topics, covering various aspects of morality, appealed to him as a Confucian scholar. Surely, there could be no harm in entering the contest.

When Xi won the contest, a greater challenge awaited him. Xi must claim the prize in person at the home of the contest sponsor, a foreign missionary. Would the foreigner's magic bewitch him? Would he find himself under the control of this foreign devil? Xi risked it for the money.

Not long afterward, he accepted a position as a Chinese tutor for the foreign missionary, David Hill. Xi observed Hill and his Christian coworkers' daily lives. Though he saw their care for the opium addicts that came to them for help, the proud Confucian shunned their prayer meetings and worship services. However, the Chinese Bible placed in his room caught his attention. At first, his interest was merely academic. As a scholar he needed to be familiar with this text since his student asked questions about it. Soon, the story of Christ captured his imagination and spoke to the needs of his heart. The more he read, the greater his sin and helplessness seemed. Finally, Xi believed on Christ. He later testified: "In earlier years men honored me as a scholarly disciple of Confucius; but I knew, with inner shame, how little the title was deserved. Now, in the truth of God, I have found the one power that alone can change the heart." [4] Those around Xi immediately noticed his transformation.

Conflict erupted without and within. First, his wife and stepmother berated him for foolishly succumbing to the foreigner's sorcery. Second, Xi knew he could not continue smoking opium. He saw a connection between drug addiction and the work of the devil. After years of addiction, this was a battle for his life. Xi cried out in pain: "Devil, what can you do against me? My life is in the hand of God. And truly I am willing to break off opium and die, but not willing to continue in sin and live!"[5] Through the trial of his withdrawal, Xi learned to pray and depend on his newfound Savior.

Once his body recovered, Xi sought to teach opium addicts what God had taught him. He later wrote, "I see now why I was permitted to pass through such a severe ordeal. It was in order that I might thoroughly understand the true nature of the conflict and the only power that can deliver."[6] Xi also changed his name to Xi Shengmo (席勝魔), which meant "defeating the devil."[7] He was convinced that only through the power of Christ was his soul saved and body delivered from the dominion of the evil one.

As Xi grew in Christ, the authenticity of his testimony impressed those around him. His wife dropped her opposition, turned to Christ, and became his partner in ministry.[8] A new missionary to Shanxi, D. E. Hoste, witnessed Xi's transformation: "The more one saw of him . . . the more one felt that Christ had taken possession of his life—the real Christ, the living Christ. Nothing else, nothing less, could have accounted for the change that came over him from that hour."[9] The slave to opium had become a servant of God.

Though young in the faith, Xi joined the ongoing outreach to opium addicts known as "the opium refuge." However, when the missionaries were away, the opium refuge ran out of the imported medicine used to ease their patients' withdrawal symptoms. Xi prayed to God for wisdom. Then, using his knowledge of traditional Chinese medicine, he concocted his own remedy.[10] When the new treatment worked, Xi insisted that God had guided his hands.[11]

Local opposition to Christianity and challenges beyond their expertise drove Xi, his wife, and their team to prayer. Former coworkers from the opium refuge backstabbed him and set up competing clinics using his own prescription. Skeptical addicts did not follow instructions and relapsed. Demoniacs, not uncommon in a society so long without God, disrupted the work.[12] Xi wrote of his source of strength against the darkness:

> On account of many onslaughts of Satan, my wife and I for the space of three years seldom put off our clothing to go to sleep, in order that we might be the more ready to watch and pray. Sometimes in a solitary place, I spent whole nights in prayer.... We had always endeavored in our thoughts, words, and actions to be well pleasing to the Lord; but now we realized more than ever our own weakness; that we were indeed nothing; and that only in seeking to do God's will, whether in working or resting, whether in peace or peril, in abundance or in want, everywhere and at all times relying on the Holy Spirit, we might accomplish the work the Lord has appointed us to do.[13]

A spirit of prayer and dependence on God permeated Xi's work.

Xi's work among the addicts spread from city to city across Shanxi.[14] Addicts flocked to the opium refuges. Most recovered from their addiction. Many believed the gospel, and new churches sprang up across the province. Hearing of Xi's expanding ministry, Hudson Taylor journeyed to visit Xi's refuges in 1886 and personally affirmed the work God had done.

In 1888, Xi felt God's leading to extend the opium refuge ministry across the Shanxi-Shaanxi border to the ancient capital, Xian. This partially Muslim city, as yet untouched by the gospel, presented unique challenges. Xi heard the naysayers and knew the odds, admitting, "It is hard work . . . and there is apparently little prospect of success. But I am willing to walk in the dark with God." [15] Over the dusty roads, Xi pressed on in faith.

Darkness comes in many forms—the unknown, drug addiction, demonic oppression, discouragement, and doubt are but a few. God helps us understand the resistance we face: "For we do not wrestle against flesh and blood, but against principalities, against powers, against the rulers of the darkness of this age, against spiritual hosts of wickedness in the heavenly places" (Ephesians 6:12). What do we do when darkness descends?

We must put on the armor of God as we advance against the darkness. Spearheading an attack on Satan's kingdom will not go unnoticed. After describing the six aspects of God's armor, Paul links them to prayer and advance:

> Praying always with all prayer and supplication in the Spirit, and watching thereunto with all perseverance and supplication for all saints; And for me, that utterance may be given unto me, that I may open my mouth boldly, to make known the mystery of the gospel, For which I am an ambassador in bonds: that therein I may speak boldly, as I ought to speak. (Ephesians 6:18–20)

What is the source of this boldness against the darkness? The power of Christ. "Be strong in the Lord, and in the power of his might" (Ephesians 6:10). Only in God's strength can we defeat the darkness.

Fear not! Go forward into the fog of this world. Walk in the dark with God.

PERSONAL REFLECTION

- What would you consider to be a walk in the dark with God?
- What experience in your life has convinced you that without dependence on God you are powerless to conquer sin and penetrate the darkness of this world?
- In what areas have you succumbed to the lie that the darkness is too deep for God to overcome?

FURTHER READING   Ephesians 6:10–20

Taylor, Mrs. Howard. *Pastor Hsi: Confucian Scholar and Christian.* London: Morgan and Scott, 1912.

DAY 26

JESUS IS ENOUGH

"I have Jesus: is not He enough?"
—XI SHIMU, OPIUM REFUGE WORKER IN CHINA (C. 1839–C. 1920)

"My God shall supply all your need according
to His riches in glory by Christ Jesus."
—PHILIPPIANS 4:19

Well after midnight, Xi Shimu fingered her tiny golden pigs and fine silk garments as she sat beside her open bridal chest.[1] An ornately decorated cupboard nearby revealed more of her wedding trousseau—silver trinkets, jade jewelry, and embroidered gowns. In the early 1800s as well as today, married Chinese women, especially the wives of scholars like Pastor Xi Shengmo, treasured their wedding gifts. These valuables served as an insurance policy were her husband to die or severe famine to strike the Shanxi province again. No woman of rank would dream of parting with her bridal gifts. Mrs. Xi sighed, but she knew what God wanted her to do.

The murmur of her husband's prayers in the next room provided the soundtrack for her thoughts. Though Mrs. Xi could not make out every word, she knew what burdened his heart. One item of prayer had dominated their prayers together for weeks. Pastor Xi had extended his opium refuge ministry from city to city, but now his funds had run out. The key city of Huozhou (previously Hwo-chow) had no gospel witness. In the middle of their prayers, God had brought the answer to Mrs. Xi's mind.

The next morning, Mrs. Xi approached her husband. No jewels sparkled from her hair clips. No earrings dangled from her ears. No rings decorated her fingers.

"I think that God has answered our prayers about that city," she told her husband. Pastor Xi could not believe his eyes as his wife, adorned like a simple peasant woman, opened her satchel. Its contents shimmered in the morning light.

"You cannot surely mean," he began, "You cannot do without—"

"Yes, I can," she said joyfully. "I can do without these: let Hwo-chow have the Gospel." [2]

With Mrs. Xi's sacrificial gift, the opium refuge opened in Huozhou. Men and women flocked to this city center to recover from their addictions and to hear the gospel. Mrs. Xi herself worked among them. She witnessed the launch of a new church plant. Local leaders soon pastored the work as foreign missionaries assisted, opening schools for both boys and girls. In the following years, Mildred Cable and her sibling coworkers, Evangeline and Francesca French, moved to Huozhou and spent over two decades building on the foundation laid by Mrs. Xi's selfless action.

In June 1886, Hudson Taylor traveled with C. T. Studd to Shanxi to see firsthand what God had done through the ministry of the Xi family. He visited the growing work in Huozhou and heard about Mrs. Xi's gift that made the work possible.

While staying in the Xis' home, Taylor asked his hostess, "Do you not miss your beautiful things?"

"Miss them!" she replied, almost with surprise. "Why, I have Jesus: is not He enough?" [3]

Sacrifice requires dependence on God. When we give up what we have been trusting and offer it for the cause of Christ, only the Savior Himself can fill that void. Whether it be giving up wedding treasures, leaving a stable job, or moving to an "unsafe" country to serve God, we must make the choice to rely on Jesus instead of the glittering crutches of this world. Is He not enough?

When we go to God in prayer for His work, the answer may be closer than we think. We pray for God to send more laborers. Are we willing to say, "Here am I! Send me" (Isaiah 6:8)? We beg God to provide funds for His work. Are we willing to consider that the money He provides may come from our own bank account?

If we sacrifice, we may lack. Are we willing to risk that Jesus is enough? In Philippians 4, the believers in the Greek city of Philippi had given to God's work despite their poverty, and God commended them for it. Paul encouraged their giving with his own testimony of God's sustaining power, saying, "I can do all things through Christ who strengthens me" (Philippians 4:13). Jesus is enough. God promises His people that when we sacrificially give to His work, He supplies our needs: "My God shall supply all your need according to his riches in glory by Christ Jesus" (Philippians 4:19).

In selfishness, we naturally hoard our possessions. In prudence, we rightly save for the future. We cautiously assess personal and financial risk. Yet, as we follow God, He will challenge where our trust lies. Do we depend on Him or on the blessings He provides? When do we truly have enough? God normally does not call us to give everything away, but when He does impress on us to give more than we have given before, what do we do? When God presents a choice between obedience and security, which would we rather have? May we, relying on God's strength, say, "I'd rather have Jesus. He is enough."

PERSONAL REFLECTION

- In what ways does my lifestyle show that Jesus is enough?
- How much is too much for me to give to God?
- If I were to seek out the needs of others around me or of missionaries overseas, how could God use me to supply what they lack?

FURTHER READING   Philippians 4:10–19

Cable, Mildred. *The Fulfillment of a Dream of Pastor Hsi's: The Story of the Work in Hwochow*. London: Morgan and Scott, 1917.

CHILD-LIKE FAITH

"Faith is dead to doubt, dumb to discouragement,
and blind to impossibility."
—JESSE IRVIN OVERHOLTZER, CHILD EVANGELIST (1877–1955)

"For the Son of Man has come to save that which was lost. . . .
Even so it is not the will of your Father who is in heaven that
one of these little ones should perish."
—MATTHEW 18:11–14

"You are too young." The words rang in Jesse Overholtzer's ears. At twelve years old, was he truly too young to trust Christ as his Savior? This is what his church, his parents, and all his Dunkard Brethren friends believed in the pioneer days of California in the late 1800s. Overholtzer's period of spiritual openness passed, and his young heart hardened. Seven years later, his rebellion against God culminated in running away from home.

In 1895, the nineteen-year-old prodigal finally made a profession of faith. However, he had merely passed from irreligious living to pious legalism.[1] As part of the denominational beliefs his parents brought from Pennsylvania Dutch country to California, he embraced the teaching of salvation by faith and works. He strove to obey stringent rules—always keeping an untrimmed beard, wearing clothes without buttons, and avoiding all forms of entertainment. He married, and over the next decade and a half, he managed his farm and growing family while serving as a lay preacher in the countryside west of Los Angeles. When the family moved north to the Sacramento Valley in 1905, the young preacher still had no peace in his heart.

In God's providence, Overholtzer bought a box of used books. One title caught his attention—*The Life of Moody*. Even without reading it, Overholtzer despised this book. His denomination's leaders had warned their people against the evangelist D. L. Moody. However, Overholtzer wondered if maybe this book might hold the key to his spiritual struggles. He wrote, "My thoughts turned to *The Life of Moody* and I was tempted to read it, though I knew I should burn it! The longer I kept it, the more I was convinced I should read it."[2] After owning it for over ten years, Overholtzer finally read the biography, and what he found only increased his inner turmoil. He began to suspect that what he had believed and taught just might be wrong!

In early 1914, God cleared the busy farmer-preacher's schedule with thirteen weeks of quarantine for scarlet fever. As he and his family recovered, Overholtzer returned to Moody's biography. He read how the evangelist described the gospel of salvation by grace through faith. Then, he compared what he read with Scripture. A word—new to Overholtzer—jumped off the page. "I literally discovered the word *grace* in the Bible," he wrote.[3]

Verses like Ephesians 2:8–9 impressed their truths upon him: "For by grace are you have been saved through faith; and that not of yourselves: it is the gift of God: Not of works, lest anyone should boast." Though Moody had long since entered heaven, his testimony and clear gospel teaching led Overholtzer to a genuine relationship with God through Jesus Christ alone.

When the family emerged from quarantine, Overholtzer ascended the pulpit to preach the grace of God. Although his wife and a few friends soon trusted Christ by grace apart from works, his denomination stuck to their tradition over the teaching of Scripture. Just over a year later, the now clean-shaven Overholtzer had to leave his church.

As Overholtzer continued his study of Scripture and sought more books that taught salvation by grace through faith, he made another discovery that shattered his preconceptions. He could not believe what he read in a volume of sermons by the British preacher Charles Spurgeon: "A child of five, if properly instructed, can as readily believe and be regenerated as anyone."[4] Age five? Overholtzer recalled being refused at age twelve. Could a child that young really understand the gospel and be saved?

Overholtzer decided to try what he would call his "knickers and pigtails experiment." Rather than share the gospel with his children or those of his new church, he decided to try evangelizing children from non-Christian homes. If his experiment failed, no one would know. To his surprise, the first time he explained the gospel to a little boy, the child understood and believed. Next, Overholtzer led a girl named Ruby to the Lord, followed by two sisters. Were these professions of faith genuine?

Not long after this, Overholtzer attended a citywide evangelistic meeting. He was shocked to see the two sisters he had led to the Lord. Though he had tried to share the gospel with their mother, she had refused to listen. That mother now sat with her daughters at the meeting. Afterward, Overholtzer asked the woman what had persuaded her to attend. "I came," she replied, "because of the changed lives of my two girls." Overholtzer was convinced—children can be saved![5]

As Overholtzer grew in his faith and knowledge of God's Word, a desire sprang up to establish an organization to encourage and train churches and Christians in child evangelism.[6] Overholtzer began praying and reaching children where God had placed him in California.[7] He started using the Wordless Book, a simple evangelistic tool employed before him by Spurgeon and Moody that would become a trademark of Overholtzer's children's ministry.[8]

At first, churches and leaders were slow to respond to Overholzter's vision of a mission for reaching children, but Overholtzer persevered. A handwritten note found in his files reads, "Faith is dead to doubt, dumb to discouragement, and blind to impossibility."[9] Finally, in May 1937 in the midst of the Great Depression, sixty-six-year-old Overholtzer founded Child Evangelism Fellowship (CEF).[10] During World War II, God expanded that work internationally. In answer to Overholtzer's prayers, Christians across the world caught God's burden for the salvation of children.

Jesus Christ loves children and calls them to believe in Him. In Mark 10:14, He said, "Let the little children come to me, and do not forbid them; for of such is the kingdom of God." In Matthew 18:6, He spoke of the "little ones who believe in Me." Our Savior concluded the parable of the lost sheep by saying, "Even so it is not the will of your Father who is in heaven that one of these little ones should perish" (Matthew 18:14). Speaking to believing children in the church at Ephesus, Paul commands them to obey their parents "in the Lord," assuming they can do so as born-again believers like their parents (Ephesians 6:1–4). In addition to the clear teaching of Scripture, Christians throughout the centuries—including this author—can attest from experience that children can be saved.

God loves children: do you share that affection? God desires the salvation of children: do you seek to teach them and gently lead them to Christ when they are ready to respond to the gospel?[11] God values children: do you value these little ones like God does? When you see a child of five, what do you see: a noisy nuisance or a soul beloved by God who needs to hear the gospel?

PERSONAL REFLECTION

- What is stopping me from sharing the gospel with the children God has placed around me?
- Have I resigned my responsibility for teaching these little ones to church programs and educational institutions?
- Can I share the gospel in a simple way that even a child could understand? If not, why not?

FURTHER READING   Matthew 18:1–14

INEXPLICABLE PEACE

"[My] heart was flooded, and [my] mind garrisoned, by the peace of God, so that [I] knew no fear."[1]

—EVANGELINE FRENCH, MISSIONARY TO CHINA AND CENTRAL ASIA (1869–1960)

"And the peace of God, which surpasses all understanding, will guard your hearts and minds through Christ Jesus."

—PHILIPPIANS 4:7

Kill the foreign devils!" the angry mob shouted over the walls of the missionary compound in the Shanxi province of China. "Missionaries and Christians deserve to die!" Instead of waiting for the ruffians to break through their door, Evangeline French opened it and led her small team of female missionaries into the crowd. At any moment, the end could come as it had for nearly two hundred of their coworkers across China during the Boxer Rebellion of 1900.[2] To the women's shock, the mob parted, still shouting threats but keeping their distance the entire ten-minute walk to the mandarin's governmental residence.

"I cannot protect you!" the mandarin shouted for both missionaries and Boxers to hear. "I will send you to the north!" The crowd roared its approval. The Boxer Rebellion's strongholds lay in that direction. Pacing from where the missionaries stood for refuge to where the gate held back the mob, the mandarin ranted against the injustices caused by foreign intruders. He drew near French.

"Whatever you do, don't go north," the mandarin whispered so only the missionary could hear. From his accent, French could tell he originally hailed from the south. Was the mandarin trying to help them? What about the Empress' command to murder them? What about the Boxers clamoring for their blood?

"We will send them north to their deaths!" the mandarin shouted once again to the crowd.

"No!" French hollered back. "We go south!"

"Absolutely not!" the mandarin fired back. The farce of an argument went on for some time until the mandarin reluctantly gave in to French's demand. He agreed to provide safe passage out of his city. In addition, he gave the missionaries letters which transferred the responsibility for their execution to the mandarin of the next city. That mandarin, then, must either kill the foreigners himself or pass the buck to the leader of the next city. The women trusted that God would protect them from city to city until they found refuge beyond the reach of the Boxers in Wuhan, Hubei (then called Hangkow).

The next day, French and her companions huddled in mule carts as the mandarin's soldiers rode alongside them heading south.

"Good thing you had those foreign pistols," the guard sitting at the front of the mule cart told French.

"Pistols?"

"It was because of the pistols up your sleeves that no one dared to attack you in the streets yesterday; if it had not been for that you would have been done for."[3]

The women had indeed hidden something up the wide sleeves of their Chinese dresses—their Bibles! The mob saw the bulges and observed the women calmly walking through the violent mob. The onlookers assumed these women's coolness in the face of death came from pistols hidden in their sleeves! However, the true source of their peace was their dependence on God.

Just days later along the road south, a raiding party of Boxers caught up with the escaping missionaries. The leading marauder seized French by her long hair and threw the sturdy woman from her seat in the first mule cart of the caravan. He raised his sword to chop off her head. At that moment, the clatter of silver coins falling from the back of the cart distracted him. He released French's hair and rushed to claim his share of the money. French's biographers later shared the lessons she learned from these experiences:

> In that hour she realised the impotence of those who kill the body to touch the calm of the spirit, for her heart was flooded, and her mind garrisoned, by the peace of God, so that she knew no fear. Later on, as she thought of her many friends who had been killed, this experience comforted her, for she knew now the measure of their suffering, and had proved the truth of the words: "He that believeth on Me shall never see death."[4]

To die meant life with God. To live meant life for God (Philippians 1:21). Either way, there was nothing to truly fear when relying on God. One hundred eighty-nine missionaries and over five hundred Chinese Christians would suffer martyrdom during the summer of 1900, but Evangeline French would not be one of them.

Experiencing God's peace and protection gave French a boldness that would eventually lead her to the Gobi Desert. Together with her younger sister Francesca and coworker Mildred Cable, she would ride mule carts loaded with gospel tracts along the Silk Road beyond the western end of the Great Wall of China. They would share Christ in Tibetan villages in the Qinghai province, in scattered Mongol encampments, and in Muslim settlements in the Xinjiang province. The daring trio would be the first European women to cross the Gobi.

God promises that when you trust Him instead of worrying, He will calm you with inexplicable peace: "And the peace of God, which surpasses all understanding, will guard your hearts and minds through Christ Jesus" (Philippians 4:7). Even when all earthly support vanishes and uncertainty surrounds you, your heart can rest secure in Christ. God's peace is a garrison, a fortress around those who depend on Him. God's Word promises, "You will keep him in perfect peace, whose mind is stayed on You, because he trusts in You. Trust in the Lord forever, for in Yah, the Lord, is everlasting strength" (Isaiah 26:3–4).

PERSONAL REFLECTION

- What hard times in my life have led me to experience the peace of God that surpasses understanding?
- Have I glorified God for this peace by telling others what God has done in my heart during difficult times?
- In what ways have I pursued the path of least resistance rather than relying on God's promise of inner peace and attempting hard things for Him?

FURTHER READING   Isaiah 26:1–12

Cable, Mildred, and Francesca French. *Something Happened.* New York: Fredrick A. Stokes, 1936.

INDOMITABLE STRENGTH

"[I] feel my dependence on him and my constant need
of the influences of the Holy Spirit."[1]

—ANN (NANCY) HASSELTINE JUDSON,
MISSIONARY TO BURMA (1789–1826)

"Through the Lord's mercies we are not consumed,
Because His compassions fail not.
They are new every morning;
Great is Your faithfulness."

—LAMENTATIONS 3:22–23

M*aybe he will never come back*, thought twenty-nine-year-old Ann Judson, as she waited in Yangon, Burma (modern-day Myanmar), for her husband.[2] Six months had passed since Adoniram Judson had sailed for Chittagong (in modern-day Bangladesh). He had expected to return after three months with a Burmese-speaking Christian, but his ship had vanished. No one, whether sailing the Indian Ocean or manning the coastline, had seen the missing vessel. Ann's missionary coworkers concluded that Adoniram must have gone down with the missing ship. Fearful of a cholera outbreak where they'd been working in Burma, the missionaries urged Ann to join them as they packed up their belongings to go work with William Carey's team in India. Reluctantly, Ann bought her ticket and closed up their home in Yangon. Was this how the first American missionary effort in Asia would end?

Ann remembered the excitement of launching out for Asia six years before on February 19, 1812. She had stood on the deck alongside her new husband, just twelve days after their wedding. On June 18, 1812, the very day that the United States declared war on England in the War of 1812, the Judsons disembarked in Kolkata, India, welcomed by William Carey and his team based in nearby Serampore. But to Ann's distress, the powerful British East India Company soon drove the new American missionaries out of the country.

Refusing to return to America, the Judsons sailed wherever they could to remain in the region. First, a barely seaworthy ship took them to Mauritius, an island off the coast of Africa. When God closed the door for a mission work there, they decided to journey to Malacca, Malaysia. However, no ship sailed directly to that destination, so the couple had no choice but to circle back to the southern tip of India to find a connecting voyage. In the Indian city of Chennai (then called Madras), the British East India Company once again moved to force the missionaries out of their domain. Desperate to avoid deportation to England, the Judsons boarded the ship with the earliest departure date. Providentially, that ship sailed directly to the country that had long burdened Adoniram Judson's heart—Burma.

During these months of uncertainty, Ann had struggled with discouragement. The sudden death of childhood friend and coworker Harriet Newell had shocked her. Then, Ann had become pregnant with her first child, a girl stillborn on the voyage to Burma. Despite her inner turmoil as she wrestled with these losses, Ann recognized God's guiding hand.

On July 14, 1813, the Judsons finally arrived in Yangon, completely exhausted and overwhelmed. Ann wrote in her journal: "We felt very gloomy and dejected the first night we arrived, in view of our prospects; but we were enabled to lean on God, and to feel that he was able to support us under the most discouraging circumstances."[3] As she depended on God, both her health and her mood improved. Just a week later, on July 22, Ann wrote, "I think I enjoy the promises of God in a higher degree than ever before, and have attained more true peace of mind and trust in the Saviour."[4] Thus strengthened by God, the new missionary threw herself into the work. She learned Burmese. She built a relationship with the wife of the governor. She held Bible classes for women.

Then in 1815, God tried Ann's trust in Him again. Her eight-month-old son passed away. Ann responded in grieving faith:

> Do not think though I write thus, that I repine at the dealings of Providence. No! though he slay me yet will I trust in him! [Job 13:15] ... Though I say with the Prophet, Behold and see if there be any sorrow like unto my sorrow, yet I would also say, It is of the Lord's mercies that we are not consumed because his compassions fail not [Lamentations 1:12; 3:22]. God is the same when he afflicts, as when he is merciful, just as worthy of

our entire trust and confidence now, as when he entrusted us with the precious little gift.[5]

Ann had learned much, but her trials were far from over.

In 1818, Adoniram's ship for Chittagong vanished. Presuming him dead, Ann and her coworkers packed to leave Burma. Ann mourned in her journal:

> This mission has never appeared in so low a state as at the present time. It seems now entirely destroyed, as we all expect to embark for Bengal [India] in a day or two. Alas! how changed are our prospects since Mr. Judson left us! How dark, how intricate the providence that now surrounds us! Yet it becomes us to be still, and know that he is God who has thus ordered our circumstances [Psalm 46:10].[6]

Ann stilled her heart before God during the two days it took for the ship carrying her team to sail down the Yangon River. To her coworkers' astonishment, God led Ann to disembark before the ship left the river to head for India.[7] She returned to her home in Yangon where she wrote, "I know I am surrounded by dangers on every hand, and expect to see much anxiety and distress: but at present I am tranquil, and intend to make an effort to pursue my [language] studies as formerly, and leave the event with God."[8] Less than a week later, Adoniram's missing ship suddenly entered the harbor. What a joyous reunion and affirmation of Ann's trust in God!

Certainly by this point, Ann had learned enough about dependence on God. What training did she still need? Yet, her greatest test still lay ahead.

In 1824, war broke out between Burma and England. The king of Burma decreed that all foreigners were spies. The Burmese officials rounded up men of any foreign nationality and sent them to what was called the "death prison." Adoniram's survival depended on whatever Ann could do. Nearly every day, Ann hiked two miles through the jungle to the prison, supplying food and bargaining for the improvement of his conditions.[9] Neither pregnancy, childbirth, nor the care of a newborn daughter kept Ann from her mission.

As the war drew to a close, the efforts of the past twenty-one months had destroyed Ann's already feeble health. Bald and emaciated after a seventeen-day fever, she wrote, "If ever I felt the value and efficacy of prayer, I did at this time. I could not rise from my couch; I could make no efforts to secure my husband; I could only plead with that great and powerful Being who has said, 'Call upon me in the day of trouble and I will hear, and thou shalt glorify me.' [Psalm 50:15]"[10] God heard her prayer, and Adoniram was released from prison. Just eight months later, Ann passed into glory at age thirty-six.[11]

Through Ann's life, we can see how God strengthens His servants to face unimaginable difficulties. Each trial and triumph prepared Ann for the next challenge. Years before she struggled alone to save her husband from the death prison, Ann observed this pattern: "Perhaps it [a trial in 1817] is only a prelude to greater afflictions. Perhaps this is the school in which I am to be taught the rudiments of suffering, and to prepare for those heavy trials, which without these first few lessons, crush as soon as inflicted."[12] Ann learned through successive difficulties that she must rely on God and that He is faithful. As a result, despite physical weakness, she found inexplicable strength to faithfully serve God in the face of unthinkable loneliness, deprivation, and death itself.

When you experience God's faithfulness, your reliance on Him grows. Yet, if you fail to learn from His mercy in your trials, you may never gain the strength necessary for God to use you in greater ways in the future. As God leads, submit to Him and grow step by step. Future triumphs for God are built upon faithful responses to trials today.

PERSONAL REFLECTION

- If I were Ann, at what point might I have given up?
- How has God's faithfulness in past trials prepared me for what I face today?
- Have I learned to depend on God or am I in a cycle of repeating past lessons?

FURTHER READING   Lamentations 3:21–26

James, Sharon. *Ann Judson: A Missionary Life for Burma.* Welwyn Garden City, England: Evangelical Press, 1998.

ACCEPTING GOD'S ANSWER

"I am not to expect the Lord to answer in just the way I suggest, or think best. Means and manner and everything must be left to the will of God."

—JOHN STAM, MISSIONARY TO CHINA (1907–1934)

"And we know that all things work together for good to those who love God, to those who are the called according to His purpose."

—ROMANS 8:28

Captured! The mission headquarters in Shanghai relayed the news to John and Betty Stam's families in December 1934. Soon, news of their kidnapping by violent soldiers in the Anhui province of China spread to churches throughout the world. Urgent petitions rose to heaven for the safety of John, Betty, and their two-month-old daughter, Helen. Days later, everyone's worst fears were realized. The young couple lay beheaded and abandoned on a lonely hillside. Their daughter was missing and presumed dead. How could this be God's answer to the prayers of so many?

As John Stam had finished his studies at the Moody Bible Institute just a few years earlier, he grappled with these kinds of questions about prayer, faith, and the sovereignty of God. In a letter to his father, Stam shared what he had learned: "I am not to expect the Lord to answer in just the way I suggest, or think best. Means and manner and everything must be left to the will of God."[1] Now his father, his mother, his in-laws, and the Christian world struggled with the will of God—the martyrdom of this faithful young missionary couple.

Unknown to everyone, an infant lay bundled up alone in an abandoned house in Miaosheo, China. No villager dared come near the home of the foreigners. The bitter December wind forced its way through the cracks in the walls and around the windows sills. For over twenty-four hours, a hungry little voice cried out, but no one would help her. No one but God.

Meanwhile, a local evangelist heard rumors of the Stams' execution. Evangelist Lo boldly entered Miaosheo to investigate. The villagers, knowing Lo's association with the foreigners and fearing the return of the soldiers, told him nothing. Then, as Lo trudged out of the village, an elderly woman furtively pointed to an empty house. He entered, wondering what horrors he would find. There lay baby Helen, still snugly wrapped as her mother had left her the day before.

Yet, John and Betty's family and friends knew nothing of the rescue. They grieved in ignorance of God's miracle. Nearly one week later—after Lo and his wife had carried Helen through war-torn Anhui to a mission station away from the conflict—the news reached Betty's parents. Her father wrote, "Everything about her [baby Helen's] deliverance tells of God's love and power. And we know that if He could bring a tiny, helpless infant, not three months old, through such dangers in perfect safety, He could no less surely have saved the lives of her precious parents, had that been in His divine plan for them."[2] The Stams' relatives chose to accept God's sovereignty.

Why were the parents killed but their daughter spared? Why does God allow the senseless killing of innocent people? Is God really in control? In times of tragedy, these kinds of questions often plague our minds. When they do, we must trust the character and promises of God.

As the psalmist testifies, "Truly God is good," and He does good (Psalm 73:1). Psalm 34:8 encourages those facing overwhelming difficulties: "Oh, taste and see that the Lord is good; Blessed is the man who trusts in Him!" From Genesis to Revelation, the Scriptures attest to the impeccability of God's character: "He is the Rock, His work is perfect; for all His ways are justice, a God of truth and without injustice; righteous and upright is He" (Deuteronomy 32:4). "God is light and in Him is no darkness at all," so God's character is completely and only good (1 John 1:5). His judgments are righteous (Revelation 19:4). Because of His unchanging nature, we can trust the God of all the earth to do right (Genesis 18:25).

When horrific circumstances seem to contradict the truth of God's goodness, the biblical account of the patriarch Joseph can provide a real-life glimpse into how God's goodness triumphs over the depraved intent of evil people. For thirteen years, while Joseph suffered gross injustice, he did not know God's plan. His spirit must have struggled against the seemingly pointless trials of his life. Why did a good God not intervene on behalf of this innocent young man? Yet, throughout Joseph's afflictions, the Lord was quietly with him (Genesis 39:3, 23). Years later, when God gave him the unusual opportunity of seeing the purpose of his suffering, Joseph confronted his first oppressors and testified of God's sovereign goodness: "You meant evil against me; but God meant it for good, in order to bring it about as it is this day, to save many people alive" (Genesis 50:20). Even if we never see the purpose of our suffering during our lifetimes, God is good and orchestrates good, even in the chaos.

When seemingly senseless tragedy shakes your world, look to God for wisdom and guidance. With the psalmist, pray, "Cause me to hear Your lovingkindness in the morning, For in You do I trust; Cause me to know the way in which I should walk, For I lift up my soul to You. . . . Teach me to do Your will, For You are my God; Your Spirit is good. Lead me in the land of uprightness" (Psalm 143:8–10). Learn to trust the sovereignty of God. You are not in control, but He is. When God does not answer your prayers in the ways you desire, believe that He knows what is best. God promises that "all things work together for good to those who love God, to those who are the called according to His purpose" (Romans 8:28). Submit to God's purposes and continue loving Him, no matter what His plan entails.

Job's godly response while reeling from the devastation of unexplained tragedy serves as an excellent example for God's people today: "The Lord gave, and the Lord has taken away; blessed be the name of the Lord" (Job 1:21).[3] Rest in God's sovereign goodness both when He gives—like when He joyously delivered baby

Helen Stam—and also when He takes—as when He allowed the infant's parents' sudden departure to their heavenly home. In either case, God is good and will bring good, though it may not be evident right away.

Our all-wise God knows what He is doing. He makes no mistakes in what He allows. Depend on Him. Find the rays of God's goodness as they shine through the darkness of an evil world. Seize that hope and refuse to let fear and doubt hinder your path of service to God.

PERSONAL REFLECTION

- In what ways has God recently reminded me that I am not in control?
- What areas of my life have I not submitted to God's sovereign and loving control? Am I nervous about what God might do if I surrendered these to Him?
- How has fear of what God might allow in my life affected my decisions of how, when, or where I should serve Him?

FURTHER READING   Psalm 143

Taylor, Mrs. Howard. *The Triumph of John and Betty Stam.* Philadelphia: China Inland Mission, 1935.

QUIETNESS AND STRENGTH

"Satan is aware of where we find our strength."
—JIM ELLIOT, MISSIONARY TO ECUADOR (1927–1956)

"In quietness and in confidence shall be your strength."
—ISAIAH 30:15

Jim Elliot splashed across the Curaray River toward the approaching Waorani visitors.[1] His companions called ahead to him, warning him not to rush and frighten away their first contacts. Barely clothed, a young man, a woman, and a teenage girl emerged from the jungle. Twenty-eight-year-old Elliot should have been the one afraid. Until that point, most encounters with the Waorani people of Ecuador had ended in bloodshed.[2]

For three days starting on January 3, 1956, Elliot, Pete Fleming, Roger Youderian, Ed McCully, and Nate Saint had camped out on the sandy riverside they called Palm Beach. Their goal was to make friendly contact with the feared Waorani. Elliot and his team hoped that they could one day share the gospel with them.

For days, no one came. However, the men saw that human footprints had joined the tracks of pumas and tapirs, and they knew the villagers were watching them.

Then on January 6 at 11:00 a.m., Elliot and his team made first contact. Months of preparations and gifts dropped from Saint's yellow Piper Cruiser airplane to the Waorani below had paid off. The three visitors seemed quite pleased to meet the five missionaries. The Waorani man even flew in Saint's plane and waved to his friends below. The women chattered away on the beach, even though the foreigners could not understand them. All enjoyed sampling the lemonade and eating the hamburgers the men fried for their new friends. Against all odds, the team's dream of establishing a gospel outpost to this unreached tribe seemed on the cusp of realization.

Where did Elliot find the courage to venture into danger for the cause of Christ? Did his daring come from his impulsive temperament or his team's collective expertise? No, his relationship with Jesus Christ emboldened him to advance the gospel where no one else had gone before. Jesus gave the command to go into all the world (Mark 16:15). He promised to be with them always (Matthew 28:19–20). Elliot's boldness came, not just in a moment of danger, but through years of preparation and devotion to Christ.

Seven years earlier, twenty-one-year-old Elliot wrote to his mother from college, quoting Isaiah 30:15: "'In quietness and in confidence shall be your strength.' I think the devil has made it his business to monopolize on three elements: noise, hurry, crowds. . . . Satan is aware of where we find our strength."[3] From an early age, Elliot guarded his quiet time alone with God. He kept a regular journal from January 1949 until 1956, cataloging what God taught him each day through his personal Bible reading.

In addition, Elliot supplemented his Bible reading with biographies of people God used in the past—David Brainerd, James O. Fraser, Samuel Zwemer, Raymond Lull, C. T. Studd, David Livingstone, Amy Carmichael, and many more. In his journal on November 19, 1949, he commented on the influence of these lives:

> Remembering with profit the reading of Behind the Ranges [by Mrs. Howard Taylor], the story of the pioneer work of James G. Fraser [sic] in Lisuland. Also Livingstone the Liberator by McNair. These were read three years ago, but I can still recall the lessons learned from them. . . . "Considering the issue of their life, imitate their faith [Hebrews 13:7]."[4]

Young Elliot chose godly role models.

On April 28, 1950, Elliot again journaled about his ongoing reading of missionary biographies: "Finished Samuel Zwemer's biography of Raymond Lull. Much stirred to thanksgiving and wonder at the man's capacities and ideals, so violently opposed to those of his period."[5] Nearly a year later, on March 22, 1951, Elliot's voracious appetite for missionary biographies led him to the passionate C. T. Studd:

> Stirred again reading of C. T. Studd's biography. Oh, that God would clothe me with the spirit of that gaunt, bearded giant with the fiery words and ringing laugh. Felt assured again that the Lord is sending me to Ecuador, having no more place in the States since so many possess so much truth here. Began work on passport last week.[6]

As he read how God used others, Elliot followed God's leading in his own life.

The daily spiritual discipline of time alone with God, augmented by the examples of faithful servants of God, shaped Elliot's view of life. In quietness and confidence, Elliot's spiritual strength grew. His courage came not from his flamboyant personality but from his walk with God.

Why is it so hard to maintain daily times alone with God? As Elliot observed when he was a college student, Satan knows the source of our strength. Therefore, the devil weaponizes even good things—the responsibilities of family, the demands of education, the necessities of the workforce, and so many other factors of the busyness of life—to crowd out our vital time with God. Because of this danger, Elliot exhorts, "Let us resist the devil in this by avoiding noise as much as we can, purposefully seeking to spend time alone, facing ourselves in the Word."[7] Even good things can be distractions from what is most important. Elliot continues, "If he [the devil] can keep us hearing radios, gossip, conversation, or even sermons, he is happy. But he will not allow quietness."[8] Why? Because in quiet time alone with God, He guides us, changes us, and strengthens us.

Elliot's spiritual preparation led him to risk his life for the spread of the gospel. He counted the cost. He read of martyrs like Raymond Lull. He knew the dangers. He had seen the spears in the Ecuadorian jungle. He was even aware of the fate of the Dye expedition in Bolivia some thirteen years earlier.[9] Despite his team's careful preparations, Elliot understood that first contact with a secluded people group could lead to misunderstandings, violence, and even death.

Just two days after sharing hamburgers with the Waorani at the riverside, Elliot and his team felt their spears. The powers of darkness raged against the oncoming light. For the sake of God and the gospel, these young missionaries gave their lives trying to reach those Jesus died to save.

When Elliot and his team's friendly first meeting with the Waorani swiftly escalated into the worst-case scenario, neither Elliot nor God was surprised. God orchestrated Elliot's martyrdom as the first motif in a symphony that four years later would climax with a gospel movement among the Waorani people. Furthermore, Elliot's example of dedication to God and passion to reach the unreached has inspired hundreds of new missionary recruits to follow him as he followed Christ (1 Corinthians 11:1).

Does your heart yearn for God to use you? Then take your time with God seriously. Set an immovable time at the start of your day, reserved for God alone. Defend that time against both the good and evil that would distract you. Shut your door. Banish your phone. Pray in secret. Meditate on God's Word in the quietness. Root out sinful habits. Find your strength in time alone with God as so many before you have done. "In quietness and in confidence shall be your strength" (Isaiah 30:15). In the silence, not the busyness, the lasting work gets done.

PERSONAL REFLECTION

- How consistent is my daily quiet time with God?
- What do I allow to displace the time I have set aside for personal devotions?
- What missionary biographies do I plan to read this year?

FURTHER READING   Isaiah 30:15–18

Elliot, Elisabeth. *The Shadow of the Almighty*. San Francisco: HarperCollins, 1958.

Elliot, Elisabeth. *Through Gates of Splendor*. Wheaton, IL: Tyndale House, 1981.

JOURNEY DEBRIEF

"Truly my soul silently waits for God;
From Him comes my salvation.
He only is my rock and my salvation;
He is my defense;
I shall not be greatly moved....
In God is my salvation and my glory;
The rock of my strength,
And my refuge, is in God.
Trust in Him at all times, you people;
Pour out your heart before Him;
God is a refuge for us....
God has spoken once,
Twice I have heard this:
That power belongs to God.
Also to You, O Lord, belongs mercy;
For You render to each one according to his work."

—PSALM 62:1-12

The poetry of King David rings with the bold melody of daring dependence on God. This tune continues throughout history as believers, like the men and women spotlighted in this missions devotional, have found that same source of strength in their walk with God. Jesus Christ has called His servants from every walk of life—parlor maids and aristocrats, bricklayers and schoolteachers, medical doctors and artillery lieutenants, and even farmers and Confucian scholars. Their commonality lies not in their occupations, personalities, or countries of origin, but in their relationship with Jesus. Their daring obedience to the Great Commission sprang from their dependence on God.

To get a fuller picture of how God has worked through this diverse group of men and women, I encourage you to use this book as a doorway into the world of missionary biographies. With this devotional, you have only stepped into the lobby of a library overflowing with spiritual challenge and inspiration. I have curated merely a fraction of what lies in the volumes listed in the "further reading" section at the end of each chapter.

In the following pages, I have also included two missionary biography checklists, subjectively separated into "Must-Read Biographies" and "Worth-Reading Biographies." Building on the lists in my previous missions devotional, *Daring Devotion*, these provide guidance on where to start your missionary biography journey.

The must-read biographies are beautifully written and devotionally rich. These gripping stories will challenge your walk with God. Furthermore, the wealth of direct quotations and first-hand accounts in these biographies will bring these servants of God to life. You may even start to feel like you know them as spiritual mentors and friends. I recommend you start with the books in this first list.

The worth-reading biographies are also excellent accounts of the lives of faithful servants of God. I have put them in the "second tier" only for your convenience. The "must-reads" will get you hooked on missionary biographies. The "worth-readings" should naturally follow. Some of these works are a little older and thus more challenging to read. Other biographies in this section focus on the historical story and share less of the spiritual or devotional aspects of the missionary's life. But each of these books is well worth the effort and will enrich your understanding of God and the people He uses to accomplish His work.

Missionary biographies continue to be written. God's work is not confined to the book of Acts or to the "Golden Century" of missions following William Carey. Faithful service to God is not a relic of a bygone era. The work of previous generations should spur you today to follow them as they followed Christ, to find your strength where they found theirs, and to further the gospel as they did. The men and women of the past can do no more for the cause of the Great Commission. They have passed on to glory. The baton is now in your hands.

THE ESSENTIAL MISSIONARY BIOGRAPHY CHECKLIST

MUST-READ BIOGRAPHIES

- [ ] *To the Golden Shore: The Life of Adoniram Judson* by Courtney Anderson

- [ ] *David Brainerd: A Flame for God* by Vance Christie

- [ ] *A Chance to Die: The Life and Legacy of Amy Carmichael* by Elisabeth Elliot

- [ ] *The Shadow of the Almighty: The Life and Testament of Jim Elliot* by Elisabeth Elliot

- [ ] *Through Gates of Splendor* by Elisabeth Elliot

- [ ] *Faithful Witness: The Life and Mission of William Carey* by Timothy George

- [ ] *Ann Judson: A Missionary Life for Burma* by Sharon James

- [ ] *By Searching: My Journey Through Doubt into Faith* by Isobel Kuhn

☐ *The Autobiography of George Müller* by George Müller

☐ *The Story of John G. Paton: Thirty Years Among South Sea Cannibals* by John Paton

☐ *Lords of the Earth: An Incredible but True Story from the Stone-Age Hell of Papua's Jungle* by Don Richardson

☐ *A Passion for the Impossible: The Life of Lilias Trotter* by Miriam Huffman Rockness

☐ *Evidence Not Seen: A Woman's Miraculous Faith in the Jungles of World War II* by Darlene Deibler Rose

☐ *Behind the Ranges: Fraser of Lisuland* by Mrs. Howard Taylor

☐ *Hudson Taylor in Early Years: The Growth of a Soul* by Dr. and Mrs. Howard Taylor

☐ *Hudson Taylor and the China Inland Mission: The Growth of a Work of God* by Dr. and Mrs. Howard Taylor

☐ *The Triumph of John and Betty Stam* by Mrs. Howard Taylor

WORTH-READING MISSIONARY BIOGRAPHIES

☐ *Robert Morrison: A Master-Builder* by Marshall Broomhall

☐ *William Carey* by S. Pearce Carey

☐ *Things As They Are: Mission Work in Southern India* by Amy Carmichael

- [ ] *John and Betty Stam: Missionary Martyrs* by Vance Christie

- [ ] *In Japan the Crickets Cry: How Could Steve Metcalf Forgive the Japanese?* by Ronald Clements

- [ ] *William Tyndale: A Biography* by David Daniell

- [ ] *George Whitefield: God's Anointed Servant in the Great Revival of the Eighteenth Century* by Arnold Dallimore

- [ ] *The Life and Diary of David Brainerd* by Jonathan Edwards

- [ ] *The Savage, My Kinsman* by Elisabeth Elliot

- [ ] *John Williams: The Martyr Missionary of Polynesia* by James Ellis

- [ ] *For the Glory: The Untold and Inspiring Story of Eric Liddell, Hero of Chariots of Fire* by Duncan Hamilton

- [ ] *Patrick of Ireland: His Life and Impact* by Michael Haykin

- [ ] *No Sacrifice Too Great: The Story of Ernest and Ruth Presswood* by Ruth Presswood Hutchins

- [ ] *God Planted Five Seeds* by Jean Dye Johnson

- [ ] *Oswald Chambers: Abandoned to God: The Life Story of the Author of* My Utmost for His Highest by David McCasland

- [ ] *Mary Slessor: A Life on the Altar for God* by Bruce McLennan

- [ ] *Henry Martyn: Saint and Scholar, First Modern Missionary to the Mohammedans* by George Smith

- [ ] *George Müller: Delighted in God!* by Roger Steer

☐ *D. L. Moody: Moody Without Sankey* by John Pollock

☐ *Hudson Taylor and Maria: A Match Made in Heaven* by John Pollock

☐ *The Cambridge Seven* by John Pollock

☐ *Lives of the Three Mrs. Judsons: Mrs. Ann H. Judson, Mrs. Sarah B. Judson, Mrs. Emily C. Judson, Missionaries to Burmah* by Arabella Stuart

☐ *Borden of Yale '09: The Life that Counts* by Mrs. Howard Taylor

NOTES

PREFACE — JOURNEY BRIEFING

1. Elisabeth Elliot, *A Chance to Die: The Life and Legacy of Amy Carmichael* (Old Tappan, NJ: Fleming H. Revell Company, 1987), 15.
2. The specific promise of Philippians 4:13 occurs in the context of learning to be content regardless of our current situation. Though this promise is written in general terms of doing "all things through Christ," we must be careful not to misapply this verse. For example, this verse does not promise that we will succeed in everything we do merely because we are Christians. The principle highlighted in this preface is dependence on Christ Who then strengthens us as we serve Him and face difficulties.

INTRODUCTION — THE STARTING POINT

1. John Griffin, *Memoirs of Captain James Wilson* (London: Benjamin Bensley, 1819), 19–30.
2. Richard Lovett, *The History of the London Missionary Society 1795–1895*, vol. 1 (London: London Missionary Society, 1899), vol. 1, 123–124. All dates and statistics in this account are taken from a letter written by James Wilson on September 1, 1784.
3. George Smith, *Twelve Pioneer Missionaries* (London: Thomas Nelson and Sons, 1900), 95.
4. Griffin, 105.
5. Ibid., 138.

DAY 1 — WILLIAM CAREY

1. William Carey became known as the Father of Modern Missions. Before Carey, churches in Britain did not send missionaries. As a result of Carey's example and the Baptist mission board he helped to establish, many other boards sprang up in the next decade which sent hundreds of new missionaries across the world.

2. John Clark Marshman, *The Life and Times of Carey, Marshman, and Ward*, vol. 1 (London: Longman, Brown, Green, Longmans, and Roberts, 1859), 65.

3. *Brief Narrative of the Baptist Mission in India* (London: Button and Son, 1810), 14.

4. William Carey, *The Journal and Selected Letters of William Carey*, Terry G. Carter, ed. (Macon, GA: Smyth and Helwys, 2000), 9.

5. Eustace Carey, *Memoir of William Carey* (Boston: Gould, Kendall and Lincoln, 1836), 113.

6. Ibid.

7. On June 12, 1806, Carey described the beginning of his typical day: "I rose this day at a quarter before six, read a chapter in the Hebrew Bible, and spent the time till seven in private addresses [in prayer] to God and then attended family prayer with the servants in Bengalee." Letter to John Ryland quoted in Timothy George, *Faithful Witness: The Life and Mission of William Carey* (Birmingham, AL: Christian History Institute, 1998), 147.

8. Marshman, 89.

9. The mission societies inspired by Carey's work included the London Missionary Society (1795), the Scottish and Glasgow Missionary Societies (1796), the Church Missionary Society (1799), the Religious Tract Society (1799), and the British and Foreign Bible Society (1804). Across the Atlantic, Samuel Mills would push for the founding of the American Board of Commissioners for Foreign Missions (1810) which soon thereafter sent out Adoniram Judson, the first American sent as a foreign missionary.

10. See also Psalm 16:5; 119:57; and 142:5.

DAY 2 — HENRY NOTT

1. Lovett, *The History of the London Missionary Society 1795–1895*, vol. 1, 152. This quotation is from a letter dated March 29, 1798, jointly signed by Henry Nott, John Jefferson, John Eyre, Henry Bicknell, John Harris, and Thomas Lewis.

2. Ibid., 134. The ship carried a total of thirty-nine passengers—thirty men, six women, and three children. The remaining passengers went on to serve God in Tonga and the Marquesas Islands. Of those who landed in Tahiti, eighteen were men, and six were women.

3. Ibid., 151.

4. Ibid., 191.

5. Ibid., 193.

6. Ibid., 802.

7. When they sent the first group of missionaries, the LMS prioritized practical skills over spiritual qualifications. They had mixed the biblical command to "go into all the world and preach the gospel" (Mark 16:15) with the cultural outlook of eighteenth-century Europe. Their dual aim of evangelization and civilization would hinder the Great Commission work.

8. Ibid., 177.

9. Eugene Myers Harrison, *Giants of the Missionary Trail* (Chicago: Scripture Press, 1954), 6. The axes, knives, and scissors were practical items brought by Europeans that the locals of Tahiti valued.
10. Lovett, The History of the London Missionary Society, 187.
11. Harrison, 20.
12. Lovett, *The History of the London Missionary Society*, 161. The mention of "appointed means" may indicate the influence of Carey's pamphlet, *An Inquiry into the Obligation of Christians to Use Means for the Conversion of the Heathen.*
13. Ibid., 206.
14. Ibid., 220–229. The testimony of Pomare caused Nott and his coworkers much concern. Though he gave a clear confession of faith in Christ, he often lapsed into drunkenness and immorality. He would also revert to despotic habits of ruling the island. However, his influence in leading his people to Christ was great. Pomare did not have much time to grow in Christ. He died in December 7, 1821, just over two years after his baptism.
15. Ibid., 214. Since Captain Cook's visit in 1769 nearly fifty years before, the population of Tahiti had plummeted. The Tahitians own destructive practices as well as imported diseases contracted from profligate European sailors contributed to this decline.
16. Ibid., 152.

DAY 3 — ERNIE PRESSWOOD

1. Ruth Presswood Hutchins, *No Sacrifice Too Great* (Chicago: Moody Publishers, 1993), 27.
2. Ibid., 28.
3. Ibid., 202.
4. Ibid., 28–29.
5. Presswood initially went to Indonesia as a single man in 1930. During his first furlough in 1935, Presswood married Laura Harmon. She died after a miscarriage in May 1938. Ernie had met Ruth in 1930 before heading to Indonesia. While on furlough in 1940, he reconnected with Ruth and after some months asked her to marry him. They wed on December 11, 1940, and sailed for Asia on May 3, 1941.
6. Read more of what God did in both the men's and especially the women's internment camps in Indonesia in Darlene Deibler Rose's book, *Evidence Not Seen.* I recommend reading Rose's book first and then supplementing it with Ruth Hutchins' book, *No Sacrifice Too Great.*
7. Ibid., 193.
8. He discovered that the Japanese had converted the house he had built into their headquarters. The invaders had also murdered his missionary coworker.
9. Ibid., 202.
10. Ibid., 132.
11. Ibid., 204.

DAY 4 — LILIAS TROTTER

1. Miriam Huffman Rockness, *A Passion for the Impossible: The Life of Lilias Trotter* (Grand Rapids, MI: Discovery House, 2003), 184–185.
2. This was one of the early meetings of what became the Keswick Movement.
3. Rockness, 66–67.
4. Ibid., 65. Her role as a substitute teacher of a Bible class quickly evolved into a full-time position. Her work expanded as she reached out to underprivileged working women and prostitutes in London.
5. Ibid., 98.
6. Ibid., 180, 251. Since the Arab women were sequestered in their homes, Trotter would get to know their boys and girls playing in the streets first, which often led to invitations into the women's homes. She also taught the women to read. She explained in a letter dated February 2, 1900: "It will be such a thing when they can get their spiritual food straight from Him through His word, instead of these scraps of oral teaching, so half remembered with their untrained memories." She also opened craft shops where women could learn a trade to earn money and escape abusive family situations.
7. Blanche A. F. Piggott, *Lilias Trotter: Founder of the Algiers Mission Band* (London: Marshall, Morgan, and Scott, 1930), 23, 43.
8. Rockness, 147. Journal entry from 1895 while Trotter convalesced in England.
9. Ibid., 156. Journal entry May 22, 1899.
10. Ibid., 186–187. Journal entry August 22, 1901. Capitalization in original.
11. Ibid., 199. Journal entry January 5, 1905.
12. Ibid., 199. "The same lesson reiterated all round by God—the simple A.B.C. lesson that where inadequacy & inefficiency on the human side are His conditions for working, 'He sealeth up the hand of every man, that all men may know His work.'" Journal entry February 23, 1905.
13. Ibid., 172.
14. Ibid., 177. Journal entry August 25, 1900.
15. During her normal schedule in Algeria, Trotter prioritized her walk with God. Whether at ease or under pressure, she guarded her daily time with God each morning from 7:15 to 8:30 (Rockness, 119). During this time, she would read the Bible and often *Daily Light*, a devotional book of topical Scripture readings (Rockness, 184). She kept a journal which she illustrated with her own artwork. In addition, she would designate certain rooms of their center in the Arab quarter as prayer rooms for herself and her fellow missionaries to use.
16. Rockness, 151.
17. Piggott, 104. She would visit him and his work in Cairo. Zwemer admired the older woman's vision for Arab ministry and her prayer life. He would later write of Trotter: "My best impression of her life could be expressed in two words—it was a life of Vision and a life of Prayer. Her eyes seemed ever looking upward, and also gazed below the surface of things. She was indiscourageable in happiness and steadfast in faith, and was an embodiment of her own expression, 'The Glory of the Impossible.' Personally, I owe very much to her missionary messages, which

were my inspiration and comfort in the early days of pioneering work in Arabia. I am sure the influence of her life will not soon die out." Piggott, 99.

18. Rockness, 308.

DAY 5 — JAMES GILMOUR

1. Richard Lovett, *James Gilmour of Mongolia: His Diaries, Letters, and Reports* (London: Religious Tract Society, 1895), 77–78.
2. Ibid., 59–60.
3. Read the unique story of how God brought James and Emily together in Belle Marvel Brain's and David Hosaflook's book, *Love Stories of Great Missionaries.*
4. Lovett, *James Gilmour of Mongolia*, 152.
5. Ibid., 78.
6. Ibid., 59. Glimour would pray, "God, help me to be in the spirit notwithstanding all distractions. Oh that God would give me more of His Spirit, more of His felt Presence, more of the spirit and power of prayer, that I may bring down blessings on this poor people of Mongolia!"
7. Ibid., 70.
8. Ibid., 107–108.
9. Ibid., 187.
10. Ibid., 214–216.
11. Ibid., 216.
12. Ibid., 205. Journal entry October 25, 1886.

DAY 6 — C. T. STUDD

1. Norman Grubb, *C.T. Studd: Athlete and Pioneer* (Atlantic City, NJ: Worldwide Revival Prayer Movement, 1943), 36–38.
2. Ibid., 37.
3. Studd would later give away his substantial inheritance. One gift of £5,000 (over £668,500 or $817,350 USD today) would help start the Moody Bible Institute in Chicago. He also gave the same amount to George Müller's orphanages in England.
4. Grubb, 37.
5. Ibid., 38.
6. Studd worked alongside multiple well-known Christians. He served with Hudson Taylor in the China Inland Mission. He also rubbed shoulders with Amy Carmichael while in India. In addition, Studd served as a guest speaker in Oswald Chamber's Bible training ministry in England.
7. Grubb, 132.
8. The Heart of Africa mission followed in the footsteps of Hudson Taylor's China Inland Mission as a faith mission that reached beyond the coast to interior regions where those not yet reached with the gospel lived. After Studd's death, the Heart of Africa Mission extended beyond Africa and became known as Worldwide Evangelization for Christ (WEC International).

9. Though Studd's example can encourage needed passion for God and His work, he seems to have lacked some balance in his life, especially after his children were grown. For example, he wrote, "Ah, we so need to be intense, and our intensity must ever increase" (Grubb, 215). In the Heart of Africa Mission, Studd required married couples to prioritize ministry over their home. He himself left his invalid wife in England, and for the last thirteen years of their marriage, they only saw each other for two weeks. His wife, though resistant to Studd's enthusiasm for African ministry at first, eventually recovered from her illness and became the head of their fledgling mission headquarters in England, producing pamphlets and helping to recruit coworkers for her husband in Africa. But after her death, Studd's intensity nearly destroyed the mission he had built.

10. Ibid., 63.

11. The famous preacher, F. B. Meyer witnessed Studd's dedicated spiritual disciplines when he stayed at Studd's home in 1885 just before the Cambridge Seven (see Day 18) left for China. Meyer wrote, "Never shall I forget a scene at 7 a.m. in the grey mist of a November morning, as daylight was flickering into the bedroom, paling the guttering candles, which from a very early hour had been lighting up the page of Scripture." Meyer asked Studd what time he had awakened to spend time with the Lord. Studd replied, "I got up at four. Christ always knows when I have had enough sleep, and He wakes me to have a good time with Him." Ibid., 51–52.

12. In his book, Malcom Gill quotes a portion of this poem with the following footnote: "The publication of the poem is unknown and was likely part of one of the many tracts C. T. Studd published." Not all verses of this poem are included here. Malcom Gill, *Knowing Who You Are: Eight Surprising Images of Christian Identity* (Eugene, OR: Wipf and Stock, 2015), 30.

DAY 7 — JEAN DYE JOHNSON

1. Jean Dye Johnson, *God Planted Five Seeds* (Sanford, FL: Ethnos360, 1966), 73.
2. Ibid., 43.
3. Ibid., 70.
4. Ibid., 95.
5. During the four years of uncertainty, Jean's coworker, Joe Moreno, persevered in his cautious attempts to make friendly contact with the Ayoré. Moreno had been led to the Lord in Michigan by team leader Cecil Dye, and Moreno followed his spiritual father as a missionary to Bolivia. Moreno learned to track Ayoré footprints in the jungle and left gifts behind for the migrating bands. Over time, the Ayoré began leaving gifts in return.
6. Ibid., 188–189.
7. Ibid., 192.
8. Ibid., 208.
9. In Jean's book, she speaks of her daily devotions as if every Christian has this habit. When her team finally made contact with the Ayoré, they crowded her house. Jean sneaked into the jungle for some quiet, but some of the teenage boys

would repeatedly interrupt her quiet time to ask what she was doing. When some of the Ayoré eventually believed on Christ, the new believers established this spiritual discipline, as taught and modeled by Jean and her team.

10. Ibid., 73.

DAY 8 — OSWALD CHAMBERS

1. David McCasland, *Oswald Chambers: Abandoned to God: The Life Story of the Author of My Utmost for His Highest* (Grand Rapids, MI: Discovery House, 1993), 213.

2. YMCA stands for Young Men's Christian Association. In its early years, this organization spread the gospel *among youth. Today, the YMCA is usually a social and sports organization across the wor*ld.

3. Ibid., 80.

4. Ibid., 94.

5. Oswald Chambers believed in sanctification as a second work of grace, and this permeates his writings, especially his most famous work, *My Utmost for His Highest*. Chambers did emphasize the priority of God's Word over personal experience. On February 4, 1906, as he prepared to leave Scotland for Japan, Chambers wrote to his brother Franklin: "'Go with Him all the way.' The end and aim and meaning of all sanctification is personal, passionate devotion to Jesus Christ. Keep bold and clear and out in the bracing facts of His revelation world, the Bible. Never compromise with those who water down the word of God to human experience, instead of allowing God to lift up our experience to His Word." Ibid., 118–119.

6. Ibid., 213. This quote also appears in *My Utmost for His Highest* in the entry for October 19. The publisher requested the following statement be included: "Taken from *The Complete Works of Oswald Chambers*, ©2000 by the Oswald Chambers Publications Assn., Ltd. Used by permission of Our Daily Bread Publishing, Grand Rapids, MI 49501. All rights reserved."

7. Ibid., 202, 281. Chambers often said he would "trust God and do the next thing." Elisabeth Elliot said the same thing when she described how she kept going after her husband's martyrdom, perhaps quoting Oswald Chambers.

DAY 9 — WILLIAM WARD

1. *Serampore Form of Agreement*, Article 10. This document, also sometimes called *The Bond of the Missionary Brotherhood of Serampore*, outlines the relationship of the missionary team in Serampore, India, who lived together in a compound in the Dutch colony and labored together for decades, bringing the gospel to India. The agreement's title page reads: "Form of Agreement respecting the Great Principles upon which the Brethren of the Mission at Serampore think it their duty to act in the work of instructing the Heathen, agreed upon at a Meeting of the Brethren at Serampore, on Monday, October 7, 1805." John Marshman, Joshua and Hannah Marshman's son who grew up with the team in Serampore, attributed the drafting of this agreement to William Ward. John Marshman,

The Life and Times of Carey, Marshman, and Ward: Embracing the History of the Serampore Mission, vol. 1 (London: Longman, Brown, Green, Longmans, and Roberts, 1859), 229. Biographer George Smith also attests that the agreement was "written out by the fervent pen of Ward." George Smith, *Life of William Carey: Shoemaker and Missionary* (London: J. M. Dent, 1909), 77.

2. The new recruits were comprised of Joshua and Hannah Marshman and their three children; Mr. and Mrs. Daniel Brunsdon; Mr. and Mrs. William Grant and their two children; Miss Tidd who had come to marry missionary John Fountain; and Ward, who was single.

3. George Smith, *Life of William Carey*, 70.

4. Timothy George, *Faithful Witness: The Life and Mission of William Carey* (Birmingham, AL: Christian History Institute, 1998), 120–124.

5. Marshman, 110–118.

6. S. Pearce Carey, *William Carey* (London: Carey Press, 1934), 112.

7. Marshman, 96–98. William Carey also vehemently opposed the slave trade, boycotting all sugar to protest slave labor on plantations in the Caribbean. In his *Enquiry*, he encouraged others to join the boycott and use the money they saved on sugar to support missions.

8. Ibid., 98.

9. He spent those months preaching in Samuel Pearce's church. Pearce was a member of the board of directors for the Baptist Missionary Society and an ardent supporter.

10. Smith, *Life of William Carey*, 224.

11. Carey said, "Brother Ward is a great prize; he does not learn the language so quickly [as the Marshmans], but he is so holy, so spiritual a man, and so useful among the children." Smith, 75. John Marshman described Ward as having "a lively imagination and a pregnant wit." Marshman, 93.

12. Smith, *Life of William Carey*, 75. January 18, 1800.

13. *Serampore Form of Agreement*, Article 10.

14. For example, early in their partnership, Ward preferred open communion (available to any believer in attendance) while Carey decided their ministry would observe closed communion (restricted to believers baptized by immersion). This difference, though not part of a primary doctrine, could have divided their team. Instead, Ward deferred to Carey, their leader, which showed Ward's submission to God and displayed his spiritual maturity cultivated in time alone with God. After some years, Carey came to agree with Ward's perspective on this issue. The team's relationship, based on having a "heart given up to God in closet religion," led to a fruitful partnership for decades to come. George, 164, 177 and Marshman, 214–215.

DAY 10 — MARIA DYER TAYLOR

1. She had been diagnosed with tuberculosis three years before.

2. John Pollock, *Hudson Taylor and Maria: A Match Made in Heaven* (Fearn, Ross-shire, Scotland: Christian Focus Publications, 1996), 182–183.

3. Ibid., 81–82. Maria also prayed as she waited for correspondence about this relationship and permission from her guardian to marry Hudson, stating, "Before opening the letters I prayed over them." She also prayed for an opportunity to meet with Hudson when their relationship was initially denied. The "chance" meeting was an answer to prayer: "'It is what I of all things wish and I think it is remarkable that I prayed if it was God's will, we might have an interview . . . After a few minutes Mr Taylor came in.' In the next moments both knew, by look, sense, the feel of a handshake, that love was mutual. 'We remarked' (in Maria's words) 'that if it was God's will the matter would be brought to a favourable issue, and if it was not His will, nobody wished it. It was suggested that we should pray together and we all three knelt down and Mr Taylor engaged in prayer.'" Ibid., 87.

4. Ibid., 89.

5. Dr. and Mrs. Howard Taylor, *Hudson Taylor in Early Years: The Growth of a Soul* (Singapore: OMF International, 1911), 454.

6. The Taylors' marriage and ministry would be marked by prayer. Their biographer, John Pollock, who researched their original handwritten notes and journals, reports: "With Hudson and Maria, together or singly, aloud or unspoken, brief or unhurried, prayer was the unselfconscious response of children to their Father." Pollock, 111.

7. The China Inland Mission (CIM) was the first faith mission, departing from the colonial trend of denominational missions and emphasizing more indigenous methods. By 1935, the mission had grown to include over 1,300 missionaries serving in 364 stations across China. In addition, the CIM also inspired similar organizations to form across the world for the evangelization of the interior of other continents. These missions included the Sudan Interior Mission (1893), the Africa Inland Mission (1895), and C. T. Studd's Heart of Africa Mission (1913).

8. Dr. and Mrs. Howard Taylor, *Hudson Taylor and the China Inland Mission: The Growth of a Work of God*, 199.

DAY 11 — J. HUDSON TAYLOR

1. Samuel M. Zwemer, *"Into All the World": The Great Commission: A Vindication and an Interpretation* (Grand Rapids, MI: Zondervan, 1943), 166. This quote is from a January 1900 speech in New York.

2. Dr. and Mrs. Howard Taylor, *Hudson Taylor and the China Inland Mission: The Growth of a Work of God*, 266–267.

3. Ibid., 275.

4. Ibid., 276.

DAY 12 — SAMUEL J. MILLS

1. In 1783, George Liele emigrated from the U.S. to Jamaica as a refugee after the War for Independence and could well be considered the first missionary from the U.S. No church in the U.S. sent him as a missionary, and no American mission board existed then to support his work. Read more of his amazing life and work

in my previous book *Daring Devotion: A 31-Day Journey with Those Who Lived God's Promises*, 51–54.

2. Thomas C. Richards, *Samuel J. Mills: Missionary Pathfinder, Pioneer, and Promoter* (Boston: The Pilgrim Press, 1906), 30–31.

3. Ibid., 28.

4. Ibid., 32.

5. Since the churches of New England at that time rarely discussed the Great Commission, Mills' fellow students and churchgoers were shocked by his enthusiasm. Abner Phelps, a senior when Mills was a freshman, related, "His thoughts were new to me, and uttered with so much self-devotion and piety they made a lasting impression on my memory." Ibid., 34.

6. In addition to praying, the students poured over reports from the British missions agencies and read George Whitefield's sermons. Ibid., 33.

7. The first wave of American missionaries sent by this board included Adoniram and Ann Judson, Samuel and Roxana Nott, Samuel and Harriet Newell, and Gordon Hall.

8. Richards, 70–71.

9. Dr. E. D. Griffin, an influential pastor in the Northeast and later president of Williams College, spoke of Mills' influence: "If I had any instrumentality in originating any of these measures [the mission board, Bible society, and a school for African Americans], I here publicly declare that in every instance I received the first impulse from Samuel John Mills." Ibid., 172.

10. At Mills' urging, the American Bible Society rose up to spread copies of Scripture among the French-speaking immigrants from Quebec, American pioneers pushing westward, and Native Americans that populated the Mississippi Valley.

11. Richards, 171.

12. Mills especially emphasized the spiritual plight of those in America's inner cities: "Generally the people are very ignorant. Ask them if they hope they are Christians, and they answer, 'Yes, they have no doubt of that.' Ask them whether they have been born again,—explain to them the nature of regeneration,—and you will ascertain that they know nothing of the subject. Press upon them the necessity of a change of heart,—tell them *Thou art the man*,—and in some instances they appear solemn and affected to tears." Ibid., 179.

13. Mills helped to found the United Foreign Missionary Society which focused on spreading the gospel among native Americans across North America, Mexico, and even South America.

14. Emily C. Judson, *Memoir of Sarah B. Judson: Member of the American Mission to Burmah* (New York: L. Colby and Company, 1848), 21–22. After his death, Mills continued to inspire others to go to the mission field. Young Sarah Hall read his memoir which stirred her heart for those who had never heard the gospel. She joined the board Mills helped to start and served as a missionary to Burma. Later, she would become Adoniram Judson's second wife. Read more of her life in my previous missions devotional, *Daring Devotion*, 73–76.

15. Mills' roommate in seminary described him: "He has an awkward figure and ungainly manners and an unelastic and croaking sort of voice; but he has a great heart and great designs [vision and plans of what God could do]." Richards, 60.
16. Ibid., 28.

DAY 13 — SAMUEL ZWEMER

1. Christy J. Wilson, *Apostle to Islam: A Biography of Samuel M. Zwemer* (Grand Rapids: Baker Book House, 1952), 36.
2. Ibid., 32. On his way from the U.S. to the Middle East, Zwemer stopped in Great Britain and met the family of Ian-Keith Falconner, early missionary to Yemen.
3. Ibid., 37.
4. Ibid., 37–38.
5. Ibid., 38.
6. Samuel M. Zwemer, *Taking Hold of God: Studies on the Nature, Need and Power of Prayer* (London: Marshall, Morgan and Scott, 1936), 115. For more about Robert Morrison and the Stams, read *Daring Devotion*, 83–87, 45–49.
7. Wilson, 24–25.
8. Mrs. Howard Taylor, *Borden of Yale '09: The Life that Counts* (Philadelphia, China Inland Mission, 1926), 269.
9. Rockness, 252.
10. McCasland, 328.
11. Zwemer, *Taking Hold of God*, 117.
12. Wilson, 293.

DAY 14 — HANNAH MARSHMAN

1. Six missionary families lived together at Serampore: William and Dorothy Carey and their four children; Joshua and Hannah Marshman with three children; Mr. and Mrs. John Fountain; Mr. and Mrs. Daniel Brundson; William Ward (single); Mrs. William Grant (widow) and her two children.
2. George, 124–125. Biographer George Smith writes of "her household books, where we find entered with loving care and thoughtful thrift all the daily details which at once form a valuable contribution to the history of prices, and show how her 'prudence' combined with the heroic self-denial of all to make the Serampore mission the light of India." Smith, *Life of William Carey*, 75.
3. Smith, *Life of William Carey*, 75.
4. Hannah describes God's work in producing the first waves of fruit in India: "Our gracious God hath arisen from His seat, and begun to work. The caste of the country is broken: and Satan is driven from some of his strongholds. I believe that since his residence in Serampore, he has never trembled as he does now . . . We have had four baptised, and more are waiting for baptism. These things cheer our hearts in the midst of all our difficulties. At present my hopes concerning that success of the Gospel in this place are great . . . I trust that God will soon call in a goodly number of His elect, and that Christ will soon have many of these heathen for His inheritance. We have people coming almost every day to enquire about

the Gospel . . . Glory be to God and the Lamb for these displays of His grace." Rachel Voigt, *Memoir of Mrs. Hannah Marshman's Earlier Years* (unpublished manuscript, n.d.), 30.

5. Smith, *Life of William Carey*, 89–91. Hannah loved teaching the children: "To me there is no employment equally pleasant with that of teaching children; it is delightful beyond description, particularly when the little creatures are attentive to the instruction given." Voigt, 53.

6. Voigt, 29–30.

7. S. Pearce Carey, 186. William Carey wrote on May 24, 1811, "A year ago we opened a free school in Calcutta. This year we added to it a school for girls. There are now in it about 140 boys and near 40 girls. . . . By brother and sister Marshman's encouragement there are two schools in our own premises at Serampore for the gratuitous instruction of youth of both sexes, supported and managed wholly by the male and female scholars in our own school. These young persons appear to enter with pleasure into the plan, contribute their money to its support, and give instruction in turns to the children of these free schools. I trust we shall be able to enlarge this plan, and to spread its influence far about the country." Smith, *Life of William Carey*, 91.

8. Voigt, 48.

9. Ibid., 42.

10. Ibid., 52. Punctuation adjusted for clarity.

11. Ibid., 49.

12. George Smith, *Twelve Pioneer Missionaries*, 76.

13. In her journal on March 2, 1805, Hannah wrote, "Enjoyed much in private this evening, felt a universal love to all mankind, carried all the world to God in prayer." Voigt, 53.

14. Ibid., 60.

15. W. H. Denham, *The Baptist Magazine*, London, August 1847, 481–482.

16. Hannah's tombstone at the Mission Chapel at Serampore reads, "In Memory of Hannah Marshman, widow of Joshua Marshman, D. D. the last surviving Member of the Mission Family at Serampore, she arrived in this settlement in October 1799, and opened a seminary to aid in the support of the Mission in May 1800, after having consecrated her life and property to the promotion of this sacred cause and exhibited an example of humble piety and energetic benevolence for forty-seven years, she died at the age of eighty, March 5, 1847."

17. Biographer George Smith goes so far as to say that Hannah Marshman was "the first missionary to the women of India, and indeed the first of all women missionaries in modern times." George Smith, *Twelve Pioneer Missionaries*, 67.

DAY 15 — JOHN WILLIAMS

1. James J. Ellis, *John Williams: The Martyr Missionary of Polynesia* (New York: Fleming H. Revell, 1889), 92.

2. Ibid., 34.

3. Ibid., 35.

4. Ibid., 40. In late 1823, early in his ministry and long before his influence had grown, Williams expressed his heart in a letter to his unsaved father: "My highest ambition, dear father, is to be faithful to my work, faithful to souls, and faithful to Christ; in a word, to be abundantly and extensively useful." Ibid., 52. He also said, "I have given myself wholly to the Lord, and desire to spend my entire life in His service. I have no other desire in my soul but to live and die in the work of the Saviour."

5. Ibid., 46.

6. July 9, 1823.

7. Ibid., 49. In his famous sermon that launched the modern missions movement, William Carey said, "Expect great things from God: attempt great things for God." This motto became associated with Carey's mission.

8. Ibid., 56.

9. John Williams, *A Narrative of Missionary Enterprises in the South Seas* (London: J. Snow, 1837), 144–150.

10. Ellis, 32.

11. Ibid., 47.

12. Read John Paton's story in *Daring Devotion*, 39–43.

13. Ellis, 92. The capitalization in this quote was adjusted for consistency. James Ellis, Williams' biographer commented: "Certainly no better example of the power of Try and Trust can be found than in Mr. Williams' own career; the two words might almost be called the motto of his life. By trying, he accomplished far more than he could have anticipated, and by trusting in God and in man [those Williams trained and sent out], he secured the opportunity for further service."

DAY 16 — MARY WILLIAMS

1. Williams, 142–143. John and Mary Williams had ten children, but only three would survive to adulthood.

2. Ibid., 143.

3. Ellis, 65–66.

4. Williams, 143–144.

5. Ebenezer Prout, *Memoirs of the Life of the Rev. John Williams, Missionary to Polynesia* (London: John Snow, Paternoster Row, 1846), 90.

6. From Martin Luther's hymn, "A Mighty Fortress is Our God."

DAY 17 — AMY CARMICHAEL

1. Amy Carmichael, *Things as They Are: Mission Work in Southern India* (London: Morgan and Scott, 1905), 129–134. The original spelling was "Ammal," but for clarity, it is simplified here to "Amma," meaning mother.

2. Carmichael, 130. Carmichael compares God's deliverance of Peter from prison in Acts 10 to Pearl-Eyes' daring escape. Though priests and temple women stood guard, one evening the little girl simply walked through the courtyard of the temple and out the door.

3. Ibid., 126–127.

4. "But, dear friends, do not, we entreat you, expect to hear of us doing great things, as an everyday matter of course. Our aim is great—it is India for Christ! But what we say to you is this: Do not expect every true story to dovetail into some other true story and end with some marvelous coincidence or miraculous conversion. Most days in real life end exactly as they began, so far as visible results are concerned. We do not find, as a rule, when we go to the houses—the literal little mud houses, I mean, of literal heathendom—that anyone inside has been praying we might come. Practical missionary life is an unexciting thing. It is not sparkling all over with incident. It is very prosaic at times." Ibid., 19–20.

5. Ibid., 51.

6. Ibid., 125.

7. After retelling a distressing incident, Carmichael writes, "It is not easy to write, it comes so close to us. Why write it, then? We write it because it seems to us it should be more fully known, so that men and women who know our God, and the secret of how to lay hold upon Him, should lay hold, and hold on for the winning of the Castes for Christ." Ibid., 111.

8. Carmichael argues: "Satan would not trouble to fight if he saw nothing worth attacking." Ibid., 28.

9. Ibid., 93–94.

10. Her sometimes dark descriptions contain rays of hope: "As one looks at the photograph [of a high caste Indian woman], does it not help in the effort to realise the utter hopelessness, from every human point of view, of trying to win such a one, for example, to even care to think of Christ? There is, over and above the natural apathy common to all, an immense barrier of accumulated merit gained by pilgrimages, austerities, and religious observances, and the soul is perfectly satisfied, and has no desire whatever after God. It is just this self-satisfaction which makes it so hopeless to try to do anything with it. And yet nothing is hopeless to God." Ibid., 22–23.

11. Ibid., 126.

12. Ibid., 47.

DAY 18 — D. E. HOSTE

1. Phyllis Thompson. *D. E. Hoste: A Prince with God* (London: China Inland Mission, 1949), 164.

2. The Cambridge Seven included C. T. Studd, Stanley Smith, Montagu Beauchamp, Arthur Polhill, Cecil Polhill, William Cassels, and D. E. Hoste. Before this time, mostly working-class men and women filled the ranks of the mission, but the surrender of these prominent university graduates was something new. In the wake of D. L. Moody's revivals, these young men's decision created a stir in the churches and newspapers of the United Kingdom. Seizing the moment, the Cambridge Seven embarked on an evangelistic farewell tour, preaching in cities across their homeland.

3. Thompson, 29.

4. Ibid., 36. Carmichael's observation echoed John 12:24.

5. Ibid., 53–54.

6. Pastor Xi grew to trust Hoste, saying, "Ah! Pastor Hoste! I couldn't get on without you!" Ibid., 66.

7. In 1890, a young missionary observed his mentor's prayer life: "Mr. Hoste and I had many long walks, usually in the afternoons. When we had walked a few miles we would get to some quiet spot where we had prayer together over the work and any matter specially laid on our hearts." Ibid., 68.

8. Ibid., 75, 80. This habit of walking while praying was suggested by Hudson Taylor when Hoste wrote to him about the difficulty he had with his mind wandering while praying.

9. Hoste often emphasized the importance of prayer: "Patient, persevering prayer plays a more vital and practical part in the development of the Mission's work than most people have any idea of." Ibid., 10.

10. Ibid., 95. Hoste initially declined the role, believing the deputy director was more suited for the job. However, Taylor thought differently. One coworker applauded the choice: "We needed a man who could give time to prayer, and thus get to know the mind of the Lord. I am most thankful that you have been led to select, it may be, the most prayerful man among us."

DAY 19 — D. L. MOODY

1. John Pollock, *D. L. Moody: Moody Without Sankey* (Fearn, Ross-shire, Scotland: Christian Focus Publications, 1997), 286–287.

2. Ibid., 102.

3. Ibid., 120.

4. Rockness, 65–68.

5. Pollock, *The Cambridge Seven* (Fearn, Ross-shire, Scotland: Christian Focus Publications, 2006), 39, 55, 85, 108, 263, 282, 309.

6. Timothy Wallstrom, *The Creation of a Student Movement to Evangelize the World* (Pasadena, CA: William Carey International University Press, 1980), 40–50. Moody hosted the first two conferences of the Student Volunteer Movement at his conference center in Northfield, Massachusetts.

7. Rockness, 67, quoting Stan Gundry, "Colorful Sayings from Colorful Moody," *Christian History* 25 (1990): 9.

8. Pollock, *D. L. Moody*, 277.

9. W. R. Moody, *Life of D. L. Moody* (London: Morgan and Scott, 1900), 40, 52.

10. "'I have sent you an account of the daily noon prayer-meeting I have at last got started here,' he wrote his mother. 'It is a great success, and they are starting them in different parts of the city. I am in hopes great good will come from it. They are also starting them in different parts of the kingdom.'" Paul Dwight Moody and Arthur Percy Fitt, *The Shorter Life of D. L. Moody* (Chicago: The Bible Institute Colportage Association, 1900), 59.

DAY 20 — RAYMOND LULL

1. Before the First Crusade (1096–1099), Pope Urban II (1088–1099) in a speech at the Council of Clermont in 1095 blasphemously promised that those who fought in the crusades would gain forgiveness of sins: "All who die by the way, whether by land or by sea, or in battle against the pagans, shall have immediate remission of sins. This I grant them through the power of God with which I am invested . . . On this account I, or rather the Lord, beseech you as Christ's heralds to publish this everywhere and to persuade all people of whatever rank, foot-soldiers and knights, poor and rich, to carry aid promptly to those Christians and to destroy that vile race [the Muslims] from the lands of our friends. I say this to those who are present, it is meant also for those who are absent. Moreover, Christ commands it." Bongars, Gesta Dei per Francos, 1, pp. 382 f., trans in Oliver J. Thatcher, and Edgar Holmes McNeal, eds., *A Source Book for Medieval History* (New York: Scribner's, 1905), 513–17.

2. Samuel M. Zwemer, *Raymond Lull: First Missionary to the Muslims* (New York: Funk and Wagnalls, 1902), 52–53.

3. Raymond Lull, *Contemplation of God*, in Samuel M. Zwemer, *Call to Prayer* (London: Marshall Brothers, 1923), 36.

4. Lull argued that Muslims must be won through the love of Christ, not the violence of the sword: "Let Christians consumed with burning love for the cause of faith only consider that since nothing has power to withstand truth, they can by God's help and His might bring infidels back to the faith; so that the precious name of Jesus, which in most regions is still unknown to most men, may be proclaimed and adored." Zwemer, *Raymond Lull*, 119.

5. In a tragic incident exacerbated by the prejudices of the day, Lull's Arabic tutor, a Muslim slave, was imprisoned for attempting to murder Lull during an altercation between tutor and learner. The slave committed suicide in jail. Due to this incident and other factors of that time period, the author almost did not include Lull in this book. Understanding the context is difficult for today's readers centuries later. Despite these factors, the author chose to include Lull's testimony as an example of learning to see the unbelieving world more like Jesus did rather than merely absorbing the cultural perspective of one's day.

6. Ibid., 57.

7. During Lull's lifetime, the majority of genuine believers remained part of the Roman Catholic Church, though there are some notable exceptions. Both true believers and nominal Christians worshiped together in services where truth and pagan customs intermingled. It was not until the Protestant Reformation more than two hundred years later that large numbers of true believers formed their own churches. Given the change at Lull's conversion and his writings, his salvation seems quite evident, despite some odd beliefs and practices common to his day. Though the Franciscan order has at times claimed Lull as one of their own, the Roman Catholic Church has declared Lull's writings to be heretical since at many points his views diverged from accepted Roman Catholic doctrine. Zwemer, who studied Lull's writings extensively, wrote, "It surprises one

continually to see how little medieval theology and how very few Romish ideas there are in Lull's writings." Zwemer, *Raymond Lull*, 90–91.

8. Ibid., 107–108.

9. Lull responded to their temptations by saying, "Ye have for me wives and all sorts of worldly pleasure if I accept the law of Mohammed? Alas, ye offer a poor prize, as all your earthly goods cannot purchase eternal glory. I, however, promise you, if ye will forsake your false and devilish law, which was spread by sword and force alone, and if ye accept my belief, Eternal Life, for the Christian faith was propagated by preaching and by the blood of holy martyrs. Therefore I advise you to become Christians even now, and so obtain everlasting glory and escape the pains of hell." Ibid., 109–110.

10. Imitating many first-century Christians, Lull longed for martyrdom. "I was tolerably rich; I led a secular life. All these things I cheerfully resigned for the sake of promoting the common good and diffusing abroad the holy faith. I learned Arabic. I have several times gone abroad to preach the Gospel to the Saracens [Muslims, usually Arabs or Turks]. I have for the sake of the faith been cast into prison and scourged. I have labored forty-five years to gain over the shepherds of the church and the princes of Europe to the common good of Christendom. Now I am old and poor, but still I am intent on the same object. I will persevere in it till death, if the Lord permits it." Ibid., 64. He wrote, "Men are wont to die, O Lord, from old age, the failure of natural warmth and excess of cold; but thus, if it be Thy will, Thy servant would not wish to die; he would prefer to die in the glow of love, even as Thou wast willing to die for him." Ibid., 134–135.

11. Ibid., 45, 147.

12. Ibid., 116. Zwemer reports, "Among the sixty-two books of meditation and devotion which are preserved in the lists of Lull's writings, there are none on the saints, and only six treat of the Virgin Mary. This is one of the many proofs in Lull's books that he was more of a Catholic than a Romanist, and that he esteemed Christ more than all the saints of the papal calendar."

DAY 21 — JAMES CHALMERS

1. Richard Lovett, *James Chalmers: His Autobiography and Letters* (New York: Fleming H. Revell, 1902), 88.

2. Ibid., 415 and Harrison, 144–145.

3. Lovett, *James Chalmers*, 285.

4. Ibid., 40.

5. Ibid., 70.

6. Ibid., 77.

7. Ibid.,166. For more about David Livingstone, read *Daring Devotion*, 175–179.

8. Ibid., 33.

9. Ibid., 425. Chalmers cataloged his explorations and God's work in three books: *Work and Adventure in New Guinea* (1885), *Pioneering in New Guinea* (1887), and *Pioneer Life and Work in New Guinea* (1895).

10. Ibid., 357.

11. Ibid., 43. That same year, Stevenson wrote of plans to spend the holidays with Chalmers in New Zealand: "Christmas I go to Auckland to meet [Chalmers], the New Guinea missionary, a man I love." Ibid., 353.

12. Ibid., 210.

13. Ibid., 99.

14. Ibid., 66.

15. Ibid., 484. The *Argus*, an Australian newspaper, reported, "The confirmed and detailed account of the Aird River massacre threw a shadow across the Commonwealth in a week of historic rejoicings." The article continued: "There is no denominational limit to the influence such a splendid character as Chalmers possessed. His record is an inspiration to all who wish to do their duty without regard to consequences."

16. Cuthbert Lennox, *James Chalmers of New Guinea* (London: Andrew Melrose, 1902), 193.

DAY 22 — GLADYS AYLWARD

1. Gladys Aylward, *The Little Woman* (Chicago: Moody Press, 1970), 23.

2. Phyllis Thompson, *A Transparent Woman: The Compelling Story of Gladys Aylward* (Grand Rapids: Zondervan, 1971), 183.

3. Aylward., 8–9.

4. Ibid., 9.

5. Ibid., 11.

6. Ibid., 11–12.

7. The journey began on October 15, 1932, from Liverpool Street Station. God encouraged Aylward on the first leg of the journey as she met a couple returning to Holland from a Bible Conference in Keswick, England. The woman listened to Aylward's plan and then said, "My dear, I am going to make a pact with you. For as long as I live, every night at nine o'clock I am going to pray for you." Ibid., 17–19.

8. The 1958 movie, *The Inn of the Sixth Happiness*, is more legend than reality with major aspects of Aylward's life and story altered. The true story needs no embellishment.

9. According to her autobiography, it seems Aylward sometimes employed the strange but all too common close-your-eyes-open-your-Bible-and-point method of seeking direction. At other times, she claims to have visions or hear the voice of God.

DAY 23 — ROBERT MOFFAT

1. David J. Deane, *Robert Moffat: The Missionary Hero of Kuruman* (New York: Fleming H. Revell, 1880), 62.

2. Ibid., 26.

3. Ibid., 36.

4. Ibid., 21–22.

5. Ibid., 22.

6. At the time, the Oorlam were called *Hottentots*, a term now considered to be pejorative.
7. Deane, 45.
8. Ibid., 46.
9. Moffat probably often repeated variations of this quote in his public speaking. Represented here is the most frequent version that is published today. Another is found in David Livingstone's biography. There, Moffat encourages the young man to "advance to unoccupied ground, specifying the vast plain to the north, where I had sometimes seen, in the morning sun, the smoke of a thousand villages, where no missionary had ever been." William Garden Blaikie, *The Personal Life of David Livingstone Chiefly from His Unpublished Journals and Correspondence in the Possession of His Family* (London: John Murray, Albemarle Street, 1881), 34.
10. Jabez Marrat. *Robert Moffat, African Missionary* (London: T. Woolmer, 1884), 77–78. Robert Morrison (1782–1834) was the first missionary to China, highlighted in *Daring Devotion*, 83–87. William Milne (1785–1822) was Morrison's coworker who served in both Macau and Malacca, Malaysia. John Williams (1796–1839), pioneer missionary to the South Pacific and William Carey (1761–1834), pioneer missionary to India, are highlighted earlier in this book. Thomas Coke (1747–1814) is called the Father of Methodist Missions. In the late 1700s, he initiated missions across the Americas from Nova Scotia to the Caribbean. Coke was also an outspoken opponent of slavery. John Wesley (1703–1791) and George Whitefield (1714–1770) were influential British evangelists. John Knox (1514–1572) was a Scottish reformer.

DAY 24 — MARY MOFFAT

1. Benjamin Broomhall, *The Evangelisation of the World: A Missionary Band: A Record of Consecration, and an Appeal* (London: Morgan and Scott, 1889), 201.
2. Deane, 87.
3. Ibid., 58.
4. The Tswana people are also called the Bechwana or Bachuana in writings of Moffat's time.
5. Belle Marvel Brain and David Hosaflook, *Love Stories of Great Missionaries* (Albania: Institute for Albanian and Protestant Studies, 2021), 20.
6. Deane, 59.
7. Broomhall, 201.
8. Ibid., 201.
9. Deane, 58–59. "Moffat came upon a party of Bushmen digging a grave for the body of a woman who had left two children. Finding that they were about to bury the children with the corpse, he begged for [the Bushmen to give the children to him]. They were given him and for some years formed a part of his household. They were named Ann and Dicky."
10. Ibid., 79–80.
11. Brain and Hosaflook, 21.

12. When, after ten years, a church finally emerged at Kuruman, Mary's work and prayers continued. With a stable home base and the testimony of both Robert and Mary, the Moffats' children grew to be godly men and women. Four out of their ten children—Mary, Ann, Elizabeth, and John—would follow their parents' footsteps and become missionaries in South Africa. Though living during the inequality of colonial times, she reminded her children, "We are but worms, doing what we can for fellow-worms. Have good courage." Broomhall, 201.

13. Brain and Hosaflook, 22.

14. Deane, 128.

15. The text of this book was originally published in 1913 by Fleming H. Revell.

DAY 25 — XI SHENGMO

1. In most records, Xi's surname is written as *Hsi*. The author has chosen to modernize the spelling to the current standard romanization for the Chinese character which is *Xi* (pronounced "shee"). In Chinese, the family name or surname is usually listed first, followed by the given name. This chapter will therefore reference this preacher by the name "Xi."

2. The profiteers included both the British Empire which introduced and forced opium on China as well as local Chinese businessmen who saw opportunity in their countrymen's addiction.

3. Mrs. Howard Taylor, *One of China's Scholars: The Early Life and Conversion of Pastor Hsi* (London: Morgan and Scott, 1912), 111.

4. Ibid., 78.

5. Ibid., 178.

6. Ibid., 179.

7. Ibid., 187.

8. See Day 28 which highlights the testimony of Mrs. Xi.

9. Ibid., 171. See Day 18 which highlights the testimony of D. E. Hoste.

10. He later testified, "With prayer and fasting, I waited upon the Lord, and besought him to point out to me the proper ingredients, and to strengthen and help me, that I might prepare the pills quickly and carry them to the refuge, that those who were breaking off opium might partake thereof and be at peace." Mrs. Howard Taylor, Pastor Hsi (of North China): One of China's Christians (London: Morgan and Scott, 1911), 64–65.

11. Taylor, *One of China's Scholars*, 12–13.

12. Mrs. Howard Taylor reports that the demon possessed came to Xi as the gospel light first touched regions dominated for centuries by the powers of darkness. With little training and, at times, infrequent missionary assistance in a large region, Xi turned to the Gospels and Acts for the answer. With praying and fasting, Xi imitated Christ and the apostle Paul, and many testified that the demons often left their victims through Xi's prayers. D. E. Hoste observed during this time: "'The whole world lieth in the wicked one;' [1 John 5:19] and the extent to which his terrible dominion may be manifested in the lives and persons of the unregenerate is clearly taught in the New Testament. Careful

observation and study of the subject have led many to conclude that although, in lands where Christianity has long held sway, the special manifestations we are now considering are comparatively unknown; the conditions among the heathen being more akin to those prevailing when and where the gospel was first propagated, it is not surprising that a corresponding energy of the powers of evil should be met with in missionary work today." Taylor, *Pastor Hsi*, xx–xxi. This author is skeptical of much so-called "spiritual warfare" today, especially in the charismatic movement. However, demon possession is a biblical reality, and it seems that those who lived in these spiritually dark regions of China experienced this phenomenon during Xi's time.

13. Taylor, *Pastor Hsi*, 34.
14. As the work grew, Xi grew in the Lord. He admitted his failings. As an older, aristocratic gentleman, he would sometimes lose patience and become dictatorial. When former coworkers resisted his leadership and tried to turn the opium refuges into a business instead of a gospel outreach, Xi realized that this was partially due to his leadership failings, and he listened to Hoste's advice to wait on the Lord. Pride could destroy all that God had done through him thus far. Through difficulty, Xi began to learn humility: "The devil, seeing that God was using me during these three or four years by the power of the Holy Spirit, sought to involve me in pride and self-consciousness. He caused ignorant men to address me as 'Pastor,' and I could not stop them. Some even behind my back went so far as to speak of me as the 'Living Jesus.' I knew that all this was just the devil's scheme to get me to take glory to myself and forsake the cross of Christ. Therefore I humbled myself still more and sought to have in all things the heart of a bond-slave, exerting my whole strength to lead men to repent and forsake sin, and thus yield no place to the devil. Not that I was able of myself to do this; it was all and only through the grace of God." Ibid., 143–144.
15. Ibid., 257. Xi continued to lean on his source of strength: "It is God that gives the increase. While we are ready to faint through many afflictions, he is working out in new and unexpected places his purposes of grace. The Lord is never weary and never discouraged. Oh, that we may more closely walk with him." Ibid., 254.

DAY 26 — XI SHIMU

1. The given name of Mrs. Xi (often written *Hsi*) does not appear in the historical records. As the wife of a renowned teacher, she would have been called Shimu, a term of respect for the wife of a teacher.
2. Dr. and Mrs. Howard Taylor, *Hudson Taylor and the China Inland Mission: The Growth of a Work of God*, 412–413. The story is also recorded in Mrs. Howard Taylor, *One of China's Scholars: The Early Life and Conversion of Pastor Hsi*, 199, and in Mildred Cable, *The Fulfilment of a Dream of Pastor Hsi's: The Story of the Work in Hwochow* (London: Morgan and Scott, 1917), 10–11.
3. Taylor, *Hudson Taylor and the China Inland Mission*, 413.

DAY 27 — JESSE IRVIN OVERHOLTZER

1. Norman Rohrer, *The Indomitable Mr. O* (Warrenton, MO: Child Evangelism Fellowship, 1970), 45–60. In Overholtzer's biography, the account of his journey to salvation seems to imply at times that he was saved during this time of pious legalism. However, as he would later teach, genuine salvation comes by faith alone apart from the human works he was trusting during his period of pious legalism (Titus 3:5). Without question, the Holy Spirit was working in his heart during this time.

2. Ibid., 55.

3. Ibid., 57.

4. Ibid., 67.

5. Ibid., 67–72, 76–77. Years later, he shared the story of this experiment while training children's workers in California, and a young woman testified that she was one of these first fruits of Overholtzer's child evangelism efforts.

6. Ibid., 79. "We did not want to interfere with Sunday schools. Instead, we wanted to do everything possible to build them up."

7. Ibid., 70–71. He wrote, "I had built a tiny room on the front porch for study and prayer. And now I arose at 4:00 a.m. to spend an hour with the Lord before the family stirred."

8. Spurgeon is thought to be the first to popularize the Wordless Book, then having only the dark, red, and clean pages. Later, Moody added the gold page to emphasize God and His love. Overholtzer is said to have added the green page as the cover to emphasize Christian growth for the newly believing child.

9. Rohrer, 80.

10. Ibid., 101–104. Key to the founding of CEF was the influence of Harry Ironside of Moody Church in Chicago and Paul Rood of the Bible Institute of Los Angeles. Other leaders like John Walvoord of Dallas Theological Seminary and Raymond Edman of Wheaton Seminary also joined with CEF. Overholtzer said, "The cooperation of fundamental pastors was essential." He desired to partner with those who firmly held to the truths of Scripture.

11. While every individual including children must make a decision to believe on Jesus to be saved, caution should be taken to avoid an error often called "decisionism." Praying a sinner's prayer without understanding, raising a hand at an invitation, or walking an aisle will not save anyone. We should balance the urgency of believing the gospel with care to avoid pressuring a child to make an outward profession of faith that is not an inward reality.

DAY 28 — EVANGELINE FRENCH

1. Mildred Cable and Francesca French, *Something Happened* (New York: Fredrick A. Stokes, 1936), 52–53.

2. The Boxer Rebellion (1899–1901) was an anti-foreign uprising in reaction to colonial powers' expansion in China. The riots became violent, resulting in the deaths of foreigners across China. Among Protestant missionaries of all denominations, at least 189 perished. Of the 1,100 China Inland Mission

missionaries at that time, fifty-eight died a martyr's death as well as twenty-one of their children. The missionaries slain during the Boxer Rebellion became known as the "China Martyrs of 1900."

3. Cable and French, 47–50.
4. Ibid., 52–53. The concluding verse in this quotation is a paraphrase of either John 8:51 or 11:26.

DAY 29 — ANN JUDSON

1. Arabella W. Stuart, *Lives of the Three Mrs. Judsons* (Boston: Lee and Shephard Publishers, 1855), 31–32. The full quote from Ann's journal entry on September 5, 1813, reads, "Yes, I do feel thankful that God has brought me to this heathen land, and placed me in a situation peculiarly calculated to make me feel my dependence on him and my constant need of the influences of the Holy Spirit. I enjoy more in reading the Scriptures, and in secret prayer than for years before; and the prosperity of this mission, and the conversion of this people, lie with weight on my mind, and draw forth my heart in constant intercession. And I do confidently believe that God will visit this land with Gospel light."
2. Ann was also called Nancy by her husband and in some biographies, including *Daring Devotion*, 35–38.
3. Stuart, 29. This entry from July 30, 1813, described their first night in Burma on July 14, 1813.
4. Ibid., 30–31. As Ann and her husband labored alone surrounded by darkness, she found hope in the promises of God. "Still, were it not for the support we derive from the gospel of Jesus, we should be ready to sink down in despondency in view of the dark and gloomy scenes around us. But when we recollect that Jesus has commanded his disciples to carry the gospel to the heathen, and promised to be with them to the end of the world; that God has promised to give the heathen to his Son for an inheritance, we are encouraged to make a beginning, though in the midst of discouragement, and leave it to Him to grant success in his own time and way." In addition, Ann prayed at this time: "Oh Lord, here I am; thou hast brought me to this heathen land, and given me desires to labor for thee. Do with me what pleaseth thee. Make me useful or not as seemeth good in thy sight. But oh, let my soul live before thee; let me serve none but thee; let me have no object in life but the promotion of thy glory."
5. Ibid., 40.
6. Ibid., 49.
7. By 1818, the circumstances that had prevented the Judsons from remaining in India in 1812 had changed so that moving to Serampore was now possible.
8. Ibid., 50.
9. Ibid., 99. One of Adoniram's fellow prisoners later wrote of her efforts: "Though living at a distance of two miles from our prison, without any means of conveyance, and very feeble in health, [Ann Judson] forgot her own comfort and infirmity, and almost every day visited us, sought out and administered to our wants, and contributed in every way to alleviate our misery. When we were all left

by the government destitute of food, she, with unwearied perseverance by some means or other, obtained for us a constant supply."

10. Ibid., 94.

11. Ibid., 103.

12. Ann H. Judson, *An Account of the American Baptist Mission to the Burman Empire* (London: J. Butterworth and Son, 1823), 119. Ann wrote this on June 18, 1817.

DAY 30 — JOHN STAM

1. Mrs. Howard Taylor, *The Triumph of John and Betty Stam* (Philadelphia: China Inland Mission, 1935), 46.

2. Ibid., 116.

3. Ibid., 109–110. John Stam's father specifically referenced both Romans 8:28 and Job 1:21 in his correspondence as he sought comfort in the promises of God after the death of his son.

DAY 31 — JIM ELLIOT

1. Elisabeth Elliot, *Through Gates of Splendor* (Wheaton, IL: Tyndale House, 1981), 194.

2. The Waorani were formerly known as the *Auca*, a pejorative name given by neighboring people groups.

3. Elisabeth Elliot, *The Shadow of the Almighty* (San Francisco: Harper Collins, 1958), 85.

4. Jim Elliot, *The Journals of Jim Elliot*, ed. Elisabeth Elliot (Grand Rapids, MI: Fleming H. Revell, 1978), 185.

5. Jim Elliot, *Journals*, 241.

6. Ibid., 321.

7. Elisabeth Elliot, *Shadow*, 85.

8. Ibid.

9. Day 7 tells the story of the Dye expedition in Bolivia. The parallels to the Elliot story are remarkable.

ACKNOWLEDGEMENTS

"Every good gift and every perfect gift is from above."
—JAMES 1:17

This book is a result of God's grace. God has given me so many blessings, beginning with my salvation: "Thanks be to God for His indescribable gift!" (2 Corinthians 9:15). By His grace, I serve in His ministry and have the ability to write this devotional to encourage others to serve Him (1 Corinthians 15:10). In the preparation of this book, God has provided every step of the way. I thank Him, and I thank those whom He has used to make this book possible.

On the human level, my wife Ellie has most influenced this devotional. Her tireless work alongside me in our family and ministry makes it possible for me to have the time and mental acuity to pursue writing in addition to the other responsibilities the Lord has given me. Furthermore, Ellie launches the editing process before anyone else. She reads my early drafts and often even the source material. She points out where my tone could be improved or content should be more focused. Without her, this book would not exist.

In addition, the beta readers for this devotional gave me keen insight and encouragement in crafting each biographical snapshot. Thank you, Steve Conrad, Deborah Lake, Micah Colbert, Matt Herbster, Andy Overly, Mike McGowan, and Mark Vowels. This devotional is more effective because of your input.

Following the beta readers, the editors deserve much thanks. Thank you, Chris Anderson, Joe Tyrpak, and Abby Huffstutler. Thank you, Beth and Julia Conrad, my daughters and unofficial editors who never fail to catch what I have missed grammatically. They even catch errors professional editors miss!

God has also supplied the artistic talent that I lack to give this devotional its proper aesthetic. The creative talents of Erik Peterson have greatly enhanced the reading experience. Thank you, Erik, for once again designing a beautiful cover and interior.

Finally, God has provided a wonderful publisher, Church Works Media. Without their marketing help, this book would not reach nearly as many readers. Promotion from where I live in Asia—thousands of miles from most of my readers on the other side of the planet—is no easy task. Thank you, Church Works Media, for your partnership in this ministry.

To God be the glory. May He use this book to further His work throughout the world.

SCRIPTURE INDEX

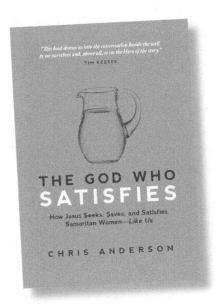

"In this little book, a gifted poet transitions to prose. I have known Chris Anderson for over two decades, first as a student and then as a fellow laborer in the work of the Kingdom. This book's focus on the Samaritan woman is full of Christ and the glorious gospel of grace. Written in an easy-to-read, popular style full of real-life illustrations, the book effectively links helpful background facts and precisely-stated theological truths to experiential application. It is a book that can be used for evangelism as well as for warming the believer's heart to renewed gratitude for what Christ has abundantly supplied."

—**Michael P. V. Barrett**, dean and professor at Puritan Reformed Theological Seminary and author of *Complete in Him*

"Here is a book I would love to put into the hands of young adults in my church so that they see that men and women who have left their mark on the mission field were like us in every way, except in their devotion to the God Who called them. We need to get rid of our lackluster Christianity in order to fulfill our individual callings, too. This book might be a brief 31-day journey, but M. R. Conrad has packed it with spiritual dynamite. Read it prayerfully. It might change your life—forever!"

—**Conrad Mbewe**, pastor of Kabwata Baptist Church and Founding Chancellor of the African Christian University in Lusaka, Zambia

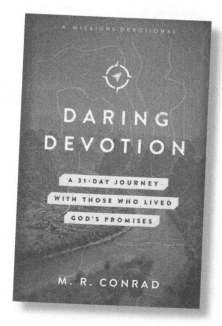

OTHER TITLES IN THIS SERIES

Gospel Meditations for Fathers

"This collection of thirty-one meditations is a must-read for any man striving to fulfill his God-given role as a father. Since each reading is both biblical and practical, it equips the reader to lead family members to greater love to Christ and to God's Word."

—**John MacArthur**, pastor of Grace Community Church, Sun Valley, California, chairman of *Grace to You*, and author of hundreds of books

Gospel Meditations for Women

"Wrestling with guilt and frustration, far too many Christian women are living below the privileges of their spiritual inheritance. The solution is not found in any strengthened resolve of duty, but rather in having souls settled in the blessed liberty of Christ through the sweet enjoyment of the gospel. A union of sound doctrine and practical teaching, *Gospel Meditations for Women* beautifully highlights those unbinding messages of grace that so powerfully ignite joyful passion for Christ and holy living. What an invaluable resource!"

—**Holly Stratton**, conference speaker and blogger at *LifeHurts.us*

Gospel Meditations for Missions

"Can we do missions without meditating on the gospel? Of course not. And yet, how many well-meaning, mission-minded saints go off into the harvest having failed to prepare their own hearts with due consideration of the good news? Too many I fear. *Gospel Meditations for Missions* helps us slow down to consider what is of first importance that we might hold this treasure more fully in our clay hearts. I joyfully commend it."

—**Thabiti Anyabwile**, pastor of Anacostia River Church, Washington, DC, and author of *What is a Healthy Church Member?*

Gospel Meditations for Young Adults

"*Gospel Meditations for Young Adults* is a breath of fresh air for young Christians and for all of us who are raising, discipling, mentoring, or just concerned about them and their spiritual growth and wellbeing. The devotionals are biblical, pastoral, succinct, readable, relevant, and relatable. More importantly, the focus is cross-centered and theological without being forced or trite. This would be a great tool to use in parenting, personal discipleship, group study, or even pastoral counseling."

—**Voddie Baucham**, dean of theology at African Christian University, Lusaka, Zambia, and author of several books

Gospel Meditations on the Reformation

"Theologically rich, thoughtful, and historically rooted devotionals are a rare treat. This volume, which unfolds the theological commitments and pastoral heart of the Reformers, is a unique and enormously helpful devotional. As the Reformers reminded us, sound doctrine must always lead to true worship. My hope is that this devotional leads many Christians to encounter biblical truth in a fresh way."

—**R. Albert Mohler, Jr.**, president of The Southern Baptist Theological Seminary, Louisville, host of *The Briefing*, and author of many books

Gospel Meditations for Prayer

"Brief and biblical, these meditations are full of sharp edges. They lead us to pray as cross-bearing disciples of Christ. Yet Anderson, Tyrpak, and Trueman comfort us with Christ's perfect grace for fallen people. So *Gospel Meditations for Prayer* is an encouraging book, but one designed to stretch you."

—**Joel Beeke**, president of Puritan Reformed Theological Seminary, Grand Rapids, and editorial director of Reformation Heritage Books